THE ORIGIN

Psychological,
Physical
and
Social

Norberto R. Keppe

Translated by Susan Berkley and Margaret Pinckard Kowarick

Campbell Hall Press
Englewood Cliffs, New Jersey

Campbell Hall Press
616 East Palisades Ave
Englewood Cliffs, NJ 07632
(201) 541-8595

Originally published in Brazil in 2000 by Proton Editora Ltda.
Under the title *A Origem Das Enfermidades*

ISBN: 0-9664302-2-0

First American Edition 2002

Interior design: John Cole
Cover design: Carlos Alberto Dalarmelino Jr.
Cover painting: Ciccione da Rapho-Guillumette

A Tribute

The cover of this book is a tribute to the great French psychiatrist Philippe Pinel, who in 1798, nine years after the start of the French Revolution, freed the mentally ill from the dungeon-like psychiatric hospitals where they were held in shackles.

My intention in writing this book is also to free the psychologically ill from their suffering, their anxieties and anguish; that is, to liberate the human being from the internal shackles that keep us chained to our infirmities — an accomplishment of the greatest possible benefit to humanity.

Norberto R. Keppe

Sao Paulo, December 2000

Translators' Note

This is a book about envy, but not in the everyday sense of the word. We normally think of envy as to covet or begrudge, " a feeling of discontent and resentment aroused by and in conjunction with a desire for the possessions or qualities of another." When the author speaks of envy he gives it a different meaning, more insidious and damaging than the way the word is commonly used and understood. Keppe's definition of envy is closer to the Latin root of the word which is *invidere* (*in*=non, *videre*=to see) equating this non-seeing to an absence of consciousness, a blindness to all that is good, beautiful and truthful in our lives.

Although Keppe was originally trained as a Freudian analyst, he observed in his earlier clinical practice that his patients exhibited an envy that was not sexually based as Freud believed, but due to a broader rejection of love – an unconscious rejection of the goodness, truth and beauty in ourselves and in others. He sees envy as the major, though mainly unseen, destructive psychological force behind our ills — mental, physical and social.

Susan Berkley
Margaret Pinckard Kowarick

Contents

The Origin Of Illness

Contents

Practically speaking, I consider this book to be the most important of all that I have written; first, because it explains the basis of problems — the cause of mental, physical and social illnesses; and second, because it provides the means to recognize and treat those problems.

For those who have no prior knowledge of my work, this book is sufficient to understand and even resolve a series of illnesses — but only if the ideas presented here are approached without preconceived notions and accepted as fully as possible. In other words, the reader must put envy aside for a bit in order to comprehend my message.

If I wrote a book about evil, it would simply be one more among the millions of pages already penned on the subject. And if human beings have not improved, it is certainly because they do not want to avoid what is bad but prefer instead to deny the good they receive, prompted by an inverted sense of values that stems from their envy.

Most of life's mysteries can be understood and resolved by perceiving envy, resistance and projection. Envy, for example, is not only invisible but also the cause of the greatest number of disastrous consequences in the life of the individual and society. In other words, our destiny is determined mainly by something we do not perceive. This being the case, we are forced to admit that modern-day science is estranged from reality because it fails to address the true origin of our ills.

When people say they want to be free, what they really mean is that they want to be free to satisfy their wildest desires without consequence, to become demented without suffering any bad results. Following one's own will means acting out one's envy, and that in turn means acting in an inverted manner (adopting harmful attitudes, making unhealthy choices).

Unfortunately, the human race is really in a serious predicament, wanting to be happy but not succeeding; thinking we know what is best when we don't; and worst of all, being seriously ill without being at all aware of it. What is to be done with someone like that?

Until a person is willing to come down to earth and live like a human being, to accept life the way it is, he will not achieve the balance he needs to be healthy and live well.

It is not that we don't want to perceive our problems, but rather that the problems themselves are due to a lack of perception. In other words, the problems don't exist in and of themselves but result from the absence of awareness. A "sick" person seems very childish because he idealizes the world and those around him, seeing things in an unrealistic, fantasy-based way. As a result, he does not live a normal, productive life, nor does he allow others to live in a well-balanced way.

When a person is not aware of his envy, his personality remains immature and he will derive pleasure from destructive acts, just as a child takes pleasure in behaving badly. This being the case, we can say that either we become aware of our fundamental shortcoming — our envy — or the human race will eventually cease to exist. Each of us is obliged to discover and work with the cause of our illnesses and to forgo the childish pleasure we take from our destructive acts. Nevertheless, pathological thoughts and feelings cannot be controlled by others — and that is a source of great satisfaction for those who persist in them.

This book was written for you, dear reader: first, because there is no human being on the face of this planet who is totally free of neurosis; and second, because if you are not willing to examine your problems in depth, your life is bound to fall very short of what it could be — precisely because the willingness to examine one's destructive attitudes in depth is the way to remedy the psychopathology that exists in all human beings.

As a rule, people are not interested in solving problems, their own or those of society. Instead, they tend to idealize themselves and pretend that the world and other people are as they imagine. In other words, the very people who idealize so greatly are the ones who get involved in all sorts of difficult situations — and because of their excessive envy, they fail to embrace and take advantage of reality, which never ceases to delight people of good will. Those who accept the real world do so because they act in accordance with their essence (which is good, beautiful and real) and because they are willing to see the errors and destructive attitudes in themselves and in others.

Personal development comes as a result of reasoning that is inverse to envy, which I can explain in the following way: all human beings have capability and talent, but what blocks them and keeps them from developing is their envy, a prior element. I can say with all certainty that if a person had no envy, they would achieve every possible success in life. In order to accept what is good (constructive), a person must be willing to see the bad (destructive) things they do, even though these generally occur on a psychological (invisible) level such as a destructive feeling, intention or thought. There is no other way to live well except by being conscious of the evil one accepts.

The purpose of this book is to make people aware of the fundamental motives that lead to all of the illnesses humans have carried with them through the ages. This is a scientific study which also embraces philosophy and theology; thus the name of the methodology I created, Analytical Trilogy. It is a book that brings awareness of mankind's problems — the only way to treat as fully as possible the illnesses that afflict our lives.

In a formal sense, we "know" everything; that is, all knowledge is infused in our inner being, requiring that we learn how to use and apply it. We reject the good we receive, not the evil, because 1) we are not grateful for all the good that exists, and 2) our enormous envy prevents us from recognizing the existence of the good things that benefit us. Our envy, which lies at the root of our personality, makes us resist good, not evil. Because of this, the greatest sacrifice for us is to practice good — a result of the process of inversion that accompanies us from the time we are born, forcing us to cling to our erroneous attitudes. Human beings in general are unwilling to accept awareness of their envy so as not to have to stop practicing evil (destructive) acts.

When we talk about envy (the keystone of pathology), we touch on the primary cause of illness — which explains why most people have a violent reaction to knowing about it. Neurosis is always an impediment to good, caused by this very strange attitude of opposing what is pleasant merely because we are not willing to see that goodness comes from outside ourselves as a gift. Because of this, the neurotic person sees anything good for his fellow humans as bad for himself and anything bad for others as good for him. In other words, the neurotic person does not wish to see anyone happy — even though in the process he condemns himself to unhappiness.

The most immediate consequence of envy is censorship, because envy is an abominable type of behavior and therefore the envious person does everything he can to avoid perceiving it. And if a person is not willing to see his problems, it's because he is not interested in what is good. Nevertheless, life is always difficult for the person who tries to make it easy.

Introduction

My hope is that this book, which explains the origin of the illnesses that afflict human beings, will be a great help to everyone so that sickness can be avoided. By sickness, I mean all types of pathological conditions: psychological, physical and social. I propose, then, that if people become conscious of the true origin of illness, the greatest problem of all; that is, the fundamental element behind our problems and unhappiness, it can be corrected as much as possible and they will begin to lead healthier and happier lives in harmony with their original sane (healthy) essence.

This study is divided into three parts. In Part One, we examine the need to become conscious of envy, the element that is basic to all of our adversities. In Part Two, we look at censorship (resistance), which is the attitude people take when they see any sign of their envy and the problems it causes; and in Part Three, the focus is on the painful consequences of projection, practiced by the neurotic, who are unwilling to face any awareness of their envy and the many errors that result from it. I believe that if readers make an honest effort to understand and accept the premises I set forth in this book, a good part of any anxiety they feel will be greatly relieved right from the outset.

With the advent of psychology in the 20th century, we began to realize that people were not what their masks made them appear to be, and that, instead, what existed behind the mask was a whole range of distrust, intrigue,

1

slander, phobia, anger, depression and paranoia — much to the dislike of the ill-intentioned and the liberation of those who adhere to goodness.

Society on the whole has adopted a delusional way of thinking, not just regarding economics but also toward politics and religion — which is why things are in such a state of disarray. People believe those three areas of human endeavor will somehow function as though by a miracle. They think they will make money by sheer luck (win the lottery or inherit a fortune) that politicians will create laws that favor the people, and that God will cause "coins of gold" to shower into their lives, figuratively speaking. My belief is that the solution to our problems is through action, as long as it is not pathological, of course.

Freud's proposal that we have an unconscious aspect of which we are not aware and that most of the time we act unconsciously, was undoubtedly one of the greatest discoveries of all. From that moment on, every notion we had about any aspect of life would have to be revised. He showed that neither was society correctly constructed, as was previously believed, nor were people as they had imagined themselves to be.

Unfortunately, due to his medical background, Freud lacked sufficient knowledge of metaphysics to see the question more realistically — which is why he did not progress beyond the bounds of traditional medicine. Nevertheless, he knew through his keen intuition that there was much more to this question than he was aware of. The purpose of this book is to provide a summary of the whole formative process of illness as well as the means to achieve a cure.

Part 1

ENVY

The chart below illustrates that the fundamental cause of illness is envy: the more envy, the less health/sanity; the less envy, the more health/sanity.

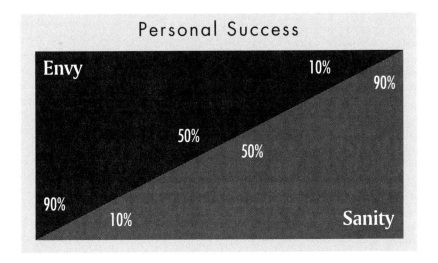

1 Goodness is the hardest thing for us to accept

"We need greater virtue to sustain good than evil fortunes."
— *François de la Rochefoucauld*

Goodness is always difficult to accept. We are accustomed to thinking that we want what is good, because that would be rational, but the fact is we act primarily in response to our emotions, and these are founded on envy, on an inverted sense of values.

The envious person has inverted values because he rejects what is positive: goodness and happiness — and then when he has made a mess of his life, he complains that he doesn't feel well. Health and well-being depend on a person's acceptance of what is good. In order to be healthy, we must be grateful, but if our envy is too strong, we will reject any feeling of gratitude.

Envy is directed precisely against those people and things a person needs the most, which is what makes this a contradictory "feeling": at the same time the individual needs a particular person, he denies this and turns against that person, preventing himself from benefitting from what is most essential. In doing this, the envious person destroys the source of his happiness and well-being. What can one do for the envious person if he rejects what he most likes and needs? This is the terrible dilemma into which people get themselves.

> ▶ *Patient (starting to cry): I think I'm still sick.*
> ▶ *Analyst: Is that what your doctor told you?*
> ▶ *Patient (still sobbing): No. It's my own idea.*
> ▶ *Analyst: In that case, are you crying because you suspect you're sick or because you see that you're well?*

We see here that consciously the patient wants to be healthy — but unconsciously she wants to be sick. I believe that what is generally referred to as the unconscious is in fact a rejection of consciousness — a theory which Freud rejected but which I believe to be valid.

It appears that our fundamental pathological behavior is to impede, destroy or diminish everything good that exists, including one's own existence — a type of behavior linked to unconscious impulses that stem from our psychogenetic structure, which is why deformities may occur from the time the fetus is formed. We are forced to admit that we carry, without perceiving it, an enormous burden of pathogenic factors that plague us our entire lives.

The primary good object that the envious person sabotages is his own life, which can be symbolized by the mother (the object) in relation to the infant who rejects her — but which in reality is a rejection of life itself. Envy, then, is the rejection of everything good that exists: it is the source of illness, of failure, and mainly of man's unhappiness. In any case, Lucifer was opposed to being (life) and thus bequeathed to us that sad "legacy."

Original (unaltered) thought and feeling are always positive. Therefore, if a person is feeling bad, it is because he is denying, omitting or distorting his true ideas and emotions. The envious person opposes reason, affection and work for

the very reason that these are the things that benefit him —
which means that he does not want good for himself. With
envy the person refuses to admit any feeling of gratitude,
because doing so would mean having to acknowledge the
goodness of others.

2 Goodness, not evil, causes the envious to suffer

When an envious person complains about someone, the implication is that something bad in the other person causes them to suffer, not that their suffering comes in fact from the other's goodness. This is the opposite of what one might think. Any good thing you do for an envious person will typically be met with fury, anger and aggression. One asks: what can be done with a person like that? He bites the hand that feeds him, spits on the plate he eats from, attacks the one who shows him affection and slanders those who help him. And mainly, he detests those who do good.

> ◗ *Patient: My husband is cheating on me.*
> ◗ *Analyst: What do you mean?*
> ◗ *Patient: I suspect he's having an affair with his secretary.*
> ◗ *Analyst: Why have you become suspicious? Has he or the secretary given you any reason to believe there is something going on between them?*
> ◗ *Patient: No. In fact she is much older than he is and only interested in her work and her family.*
> ◗ *Analyst: In this case aren't you doing everything you can to establish a negative idea about him? Isn't it more a question of envy?*

It is very common for the envious person to dig until he finds a defect in the other so that he can vent and justify his vile feelings. But for the most part, he sees in the other all of his own intentions; in this case, her sexual voracity. This attitude leaves the other totally confused, unable to understand such accusations.

▶ *Patient: I see that envy doesn't let me participate in life.*
▶ *Analyst: What do you associate life with?*
▶ *Patient: Satisfaction and happiness.*
▶ *Analyst: Then you don't accept satisfaction and happiness?*
▶ *Patient: I accept both, but not the way to achieve them.*
▶ *Analyst: And how would you do this?*
▶ *Patient: I don't know. I don't see. I only know that I used to share in the happiness of others.*
▶ *Analyst: And now that you don't wish to make anyone happy, you don't receive this pleasure for yourself either.*
▶ *Patient: Isn't that a devilish attitude?*
▶ *Analyst: You're saying that you identify with devils!*

Any and all feelings of envy affect not only the life of the person from whom such feelings emanate, but the world around him as well. What most offends the envious person is not the behavior of someone else but that person's very being. They do not want the person they envy to exist and they fight with all their might to make that person succumb. The envious do not admire anyone considered a genius and thus fail to benefit from their contributions. The greater the envy, the fewer the ideals; the greater the ideals, the less the envy — for the capacity of a person is inversely proportional to their envy.

The unhappiness the neurotic person feels, the apathy, their lack of interest in life and critical nature are all due to their colossal envy. What we call positive thinking (looking at the world with optimism) cannot exist in an envious mind. When theologians warned against the seven deadly sins (pride, anger, greed, laziness, gluttony, envy and lust) they did so because such types of behavior disrupt personal well-being. The prideful (arrogant) generally isolate themselves in their delirious thoughts. The angry have no time left over to organize their lives. The greedy live in a world the size of the dollar bills they have in the bank. The lazy are obviously unable to achieve any sort of success. Those who eat too much cannot deal with anything except their voluminous and uncomfortable body. Those who fantasize too much about sex fall into a torpor similar to that of the drug addict. But those whose envy is very strong will attack everything in life: their mind, their well being, their work, money, friends, love, intelligence; in other words, anything good — because envy is the root of all vices and all evils.

3 Envy prevents us from seeing the good things in life

▶ *Patient: I dreamed I was in a very beautiful place I had never been in before and I was enthralled.*
▶ *Analyst: Note that as you become more aware of your envy you begin to see wonderful things you weren't aware of before.*

Envy makes us blind and prevents us from enjoying all the good things life has to offer — and because of this, the envious makes their lives very disagreeable for themselves. Just as destructive attitudes (vices) lead to an unhappy life, so do good attitudes (virtues) lead to well-being.

▶ *The patient continued: Because envy devalues everything, I reject things I want to do even before I do them.*
▶ *Analyst: So we can conclude that the envious person suffers a lot.*

Another patient who had remained silent for months in the group therapy sessions said the following:

▶ *Patient: I always had the idea that my eternally silent attitude showed my superiority, but now I see it's because of something else: my envy.*
▶ *Analyst: Can you give me a better idea of what you mean?*

The Origin Of Illness

> *Patient: I see that by not saying anything I also harm myself, because in the school where I teach, the same thing happens. When I want to explain something, I don't know what to say.*

It's a curious fact that people think only others will suffer from their aggression. Our degree of understanding depends entirely upon our envy: the less envy, the more we understand. The more envy, the less awareness/knowledge. I believe that modern scientists have been so fond of inductive reasoning precisely because it gives them the freedom to link understanding and envy — the origin of all absurd theories.

Envy is like a poisonous snake that hides in the corner waiting to attack its unsuspecting victim — except in this case, the aggressor and the victim are initially one and the same. Envy is the only two-way "feeling" (coming and going) that easily deceives its originator. It is everywhere, yet it appears to have almost no purpose in life. At the same time it appears to be like an insidious little animal and a stampeding elephant, capable of destroying a whole region.

What is the worst thing envy causes? The absence of happiness in the life of the envious person and all of the resulting disturbances named in the seven deadly sins: a desperate desire for money, a voracious appetite for food and sex, a refusal to work, and anger and arrogance in the face of what is good. In other words, envy is the mother of all ills; mankind's original sin. All displeasure for life comes from the envy one harbors toward goodness, thereby preventing ourselves from benefitting from it.

If something is making you unhappy, if you are feeling vaguely uneasy, it is surely because you are experiencing the "feeling" of envy. And to better understand envy, one has only to compare it to the feeling of gratitude (a true feeling), which implies a love of life and all it has to offer.

4 The envious person is both starved for affection and dangerous

The envious person behaves aggressively, all the while complaining of a lack of affection.

> ▶ *Patient: Whenever things are going well I become furious.*
> ▶ *Analyst: How so?*
> ▶ *Patient: I see that because of envy I don't accept goodness and that's why I like to watch violent movies in which everything is destroyed.*
> ▶ *Analyst: Then isn't that a question of inversion? The worse the destruction, the more you like it?*

As long we humans fail to perceive how strong our envy is, there will be neither peace nor true development. Our behavior will continue to be destructive toward all of the good we receive, including the good of our own lives.

> ▶ *Patient: I notice how difficult it is for those of us who are co-owners of our companies to assume responsibility for them. They are the best thing we have and we don't even realize they're ours.*
> ▶ *Analyst: Isn't that because the process of envy keeps you from accepting what is good ?*

The Origin Of Illness

> ▶ *Patient: The consciousness of that fact just doesn't seem to sink in.*

The same is true for the majority of human beings, who are destroying the very planet on which they live as if the world were not their own.

> ▶ *Patient: I always think other people are out to do me harm.*
> ▶ *Analyst: Or is it that you don't want to see that you blame others for the harm you do to yourself?*

The process of envy causes a person to project, to invert the truth. Instead of seeing that he himself is ruining his life, the patient sees his destructive attitude in others.

The phenomenon of inversion in psychological life bewilders many psychotherapists because their patients a) generally attack those who benefit them — including the psychotherapists themselves, and b) by doing this they keep from being cured of their ills — so how can they get better if they aren't willing to accept improvement?

The envious see everything, good as well as evil, as being outside themselves. That is why they try to find happiness (well-being) by traveling, following special diets or exercise programs, going to parties, seeking personal recognition, or by following fads and joining cults. At the same time, they see everything bad as coming from others, from outside themselves, which is why they tend to be aggressive and generally become unpleasant to be with.

How can an envious person be helped if they see everything in an inverted manner; i.e. opposite to the way it really is? When young, they refuse to accept their parents' guidance because they project onto them their own bad intentions, and they do the same with their teachers. Later, in the workplace, they distrust the company they work for, just as they distrusted their parents. If they go to a doctor or a psychotherapist they act the same way. Suddenly they notice that life is slipping away and they haven't accomplished much, if anything.

The point I wish to make is that if one's envy is not perceived and thus cannot be corrected, it will be impossible to accomplish anything of value. Therefore, if true culture and civilization are to exist, it is absolutely necessity to consider psychotherapy a universal requirement.

5 Envy is the primary cause of all maladies

All of my work, which I call Analytical Trilogy, is based on Sigmund Freud's discovery (and the subsequent research of Melanie Klein and Wilfred Bion) that envy is the primary cause of all mental disturbances. However, I see the problem of envy in all facets of life, not just in relation to sexuality. There is no doubt that this point of view has triggered enormous controversy and indignation against my work because there is no human being who is not contaminated by this terrible malady.

Envy is the root of all evil, the father of all misdeeds. All of the world's ills stem from this terrible feeling that tries to annihilate what truly exists and which drives humans and their civilization mad. For example, the envious person who is voracious has no control over his sex drive (libido) and thus is promiscuous. The same can be said about greed, gluttony, laziness, and even about anger and arrogance.

▶ *Patient: When I play the guitar I sometimes get so nervous that I can't play well.*
▶ *Analyst: What do you feel or think when you play?*
▶ *Patient: I worry about making mistakes.*
▶ *Analyst: The fact that you pay more attention to your faults than to your qualities reveals your envy.*

The Origin Of Illness

The fact that the envious are more concerned with things they imagine than with things that are real shows that alienation is identified with envy. Neither illness nor anxiety or uneasiness exists in and of itself; if there were no envy, life would be free of all ills.

Envy is the most difficult "feeling"and at the same time the most easily resolved. It is difficult because for the most part it is innate, affecting every single person, and easy because anyone can use their will to prevent envy from dominating their behavior. That said, it becomes obvious that becoming aware of the problem of envy is the first step to overcoming it.

6

The greater one's envy, the harder it is to see in oneself; the less one's envy, the easier it is to see

Because envy is the driving force behind any denial, omission or distortion of true feeling (love), it is rarely felt by its bearer. The greater the envy, the less it is perceived. The more envious one is, the less awareness one will have of any aspect of one's life. The healthier person is more aware of his envy — thinking himself to be more envious than others. The sicker individual has less perception of his envy, giving the impression that he has no problems at all. This is the origin of mankind's inverted behavior.

Everything you see without envy will cause you great satisfaction, whereas everything you see with envy will make you ill at ease. By the same token, everything you do without envy will be successful and whatever is founded on envy will come to naught.

> ▶ *Patient: Lots of students leave our school without learning the wisdom offered there. I think they are throwing away something precious.*
> ▶ *Analyst: Why do you think they do that ?*
> ▶ *Patient: They give the excuse that they can't afford it, but it's because of the envy they feel toward the texts they read. (The school the patient refers to here uses*

texts from Dr. Keppe's work as reading material for their language courses.)

Pathological behavior is a measure of the person's degree of envy. If not too great, the offense will be minor (petty theft, slander); if moderate, the offense may involve street gangs, muggings and fist fights; if great, it may involve organized crime, serious offenses or other forms of destruction. The more intense the "feeling" (of envy) the more intense, hateful and vengeful the crime.

> ❭ *Patient: I went to visit a friend who was here doing psychotherapy and later he returned to Brasilia and reverted back to the deplorable state in which he used to live.*
> ❭ *Analyst: What do you associate his attitude with?*
> ❭ *Patient: With a lack of gratitude and an opposition to the good things in his life.*

Very frequently, when people achieve something good in their life, they throw it all away so as not to be grateful for the benefits they have received — and later they blame precisely those who gave them help. Our greatest treasure is awareness, yet the envious confuse awareness of their mistakes with the mistakes themselves. Awareness is the most valuable thing a person can attain, yet it can be eclipsed by envy.

7 Envy is the most unnecessary, useless and harmful thing that exists

Envy is the most negative element for the existence of the human being and society — an absolutely useless "feeling" which serves only to harm its bearer and others. It is totally unnecessary because it produces no good whatsoever. If envy did not exist it would be the greatest of all favors for mankind. In other words, the attitude of the envious person is to say no to all goodness, be opposed to any improvement — in essence, a way of introducing uselessness into social life.

In greed, the person uses the excuse that he is economizing his wealth; in gluttony, that he needs to eat a lot in order to be productive; in lust, that it is a way to have a more enjoyable life; in anger, that he has good reason to detest certain people; in laziness, that he isn't healthy enough to work; and even for arrogance he finds an excuse, saying that he knows more than others. But for envy there is no "justification." The envious person gratuitously goes against everything and everyone, and especially himself, merely because he is angry about what others have and even about what he himself has. I believe that with envy human beings simply do not want to be; they want to eliminate all life and goodness.

> *Patient: We used to distribute promotional flyers as a team. But we gave up.*
> *Analyst: Why?*
> *Patient: Because RL put a lot of pressure on us to work only for the school.*
> *Analyst: So you are using RL as an excuse for your self-sabotage.*

The flyer distribution team knew their work was necessary for all the businesses that employed them. However, some of the more envious team members took advantage of a management breakdown and used it as an excuse to sabotage their work, even though they knew they would be harming themselves.

> *Patient: M wants to leave and I asked her if it was because she didn't feel good living with us. In fact, my father asked her the same question and she said that now she wants to see her family, or even move back in with them.*

I must clarify that M was an adopted child whose mother had given her to another family to raise. Her biological family did not have the slightest interest in her return. She was 16 years old and her biological family could not afford to pay her school tuition and other expenses.

> *Analyst: Why do you think M wants to leave?*

Noting that the patient did not know how to respond, I suggested envy.

> *Patient: I guess there's no other explanation.*

We see that envy is totally gratuitous because it brings no good whatsoever. It is a purely destructive process; an anti-attitude; a denial of being; a negation, omission and distortion of what exists. There is no logical reason for envy to exist.

> ▶ *Patient: I was happy to be able to go and see your TV program but then I got furious when you gave an example that applied to me.*
> ▶ *Analyst: What do you associate my TV program with?*
> ▶ *Patient: It's very beautiful.*
> ▶ *Analyst: So you became furious because you were envious of the program but gave the excuse that you became offended because I gave an example of a problem similar to yours.*

The envious person wastes a lot of time trying to justify his anger toward the good of others instead of cultivating his own talents and developing the good in himself.

> ▶ *Patient: I got mad when you said that the daughter of a certain client was becoming very successful.*
> ▶ *Analyst: Are you envious of her?*
> ▶ *Patient: I'm envious of people who are born rich, not of people who have worked to become rich.*
> ▶ *Analyst: You are envious of people who have an easy life, not of those who have to work hard to make a good living.*

Note that envy is directed toward the rich, not toward people who work hard — which signifies that the envious person has no intention whatsoever of making any sacrifice to achieve success. Clearly, the envious person wishes not only to destroy what another person has but also to devalue their effort and dedication — even though by doing so he puts an end to all the good he himself has, including the affection of others.

8 The envious person generally doesn't perceive his envy

The biggest problem concerning envy is that it generally isn't perceived; it is the opposite of consciousness. Humanity is at a cross-roads: how can we perceive this most destructive element in our lives if the element itself is so difficult to see? In fact, envy is synonymous with lack of perception. And the great mystery of envy is that it constitutes the denial, omission or distortion of being, which is why not only love, but also reason and consciousness are practically absent in our lives, the result of our attitudes of opposition to what is good, beautiful and real.

When someone says they are not envious, it is because envy is precisely an absence of feeling. Since envy is the antithesis of consciousness; i.e. a lack of awareness, the person doesn't perceive it — and until they do, cannot correct it. Unaware of the source of physical, mental and social sickness, people in general do not accept the psychology that underlies psychosomatic medicine nor do they bring social problems up for discussion so that they can be resolved.

What exists is consciousness, the denial of which I have termed *inconscientization*. Admittedly there truly is an unconscious component in the human psyche, a lack of awareness. We have in ourselves consciousness and its denial, being and its negation (non-being), the yes and the no. And because denial is opposition to goodness, it requires a very intense attitude to annul and un-make everything that is good.

With envy the individual is aggressive toward others and does very foolish things without realizing it. And since envy cannot be perceived, it takes an act of faith for the person to admit its existence. Indeed, the greatest obstacle to accepting one's envy is precisely its invisibility, as if it were a hidden demon. It is as if the devil, who characterizes envy, becomes so ashamed of this feeling that he hides himself in order not to reveal it. Everything we fail to perceive is due to our envy.

Envy is more easily perceived indirectly, through its consequences; for example, in the voracity that the envious have for food, money, sex and other people's possessions; and in their anger, laziness and arrogance. The less genuine feeling (affection) a person has, the more envious that person is. And since envy is an absence of true feeling (love), a person does not easily perceive it until he shows love and then all of his negative "feelings" appear, causing him great suffering.

> *Patient: Yesterday I felt anxious and I didn't know why. Saturday I went to the ballet and didn't feel well. I work with a teacher at the language school and I don't think the environment there is very good.*
> *Analyst: You're only interested in what makes you happy and don't make an effort to see the things that are truly important in your life. Sometimes what makes us unhappy is more valuable than the things that make us happy. If you believe you're unhappy because of something good, it's a sign you're headed in the wrong direction.*

I would like to clarify here that we can be misguided in our search for happiness. The most important thing is to know and do what is right, which is not necessarily what brings us the most satisfaction. In fact, it is by doing good that one perceives all of the evil that exists inside oneself — and obviously this is not pleasant. By adopting a good attitude, we become able to see our bad attitudes, but if we keep doing what is harmful we will remain blind to what is good.

The more good we receive, the greater our resistance to recognizing it. In psychotherapy this fact becomes glaringly evident, for in acknowledging the good received, the person would at the same time have to admit their cunning opposition to goodness, truth and life — and in order not to admit their malice, they also deny the good they themselves possess.

> ▶ *Patient: When I was doing analysis I suffered a lot.*
> ▶ *Analyst: Or was it that while you were getting the benefit of analysis you were also forced to see your bad attitude?*

The main reason we should accept goodness is that it is a beacon that illuminates all the bad attitudes that exist in the world and in those willing to analyze themselves.

9 If envy is an unwillingness to see, how can one see it?

If envy is the act of not wanting to see, and if it blinds the envious person to the world (to its problems as well as its beauty), how can it be seen by the envious individual? And if everyone suffers from this terrible "feeling," how can we improve our psychological and social life? Humanity must resolve this great dilemma if it is to regain sanity.

> *Patient: I'm always dissatisfied, never content to be where I am.*
> *Analyst: That is one of the signs of envy.*
> *Patient: Envy is hard to perceive.*

Since envy is the opposite of awareness, it cannot be entirely perceived except by its consequences. And because of this, we are open to all sorts of destructive behavior: greed, gluttony, arrogance and such. In this way, we become victims of something we don't clearly see.

> *Patient: I'm trying to see my problems, as you suggested.*
> *Analyst: Can you give me an example?*
> *Patient: In England I sabotaged my work as an analyst.*
> *Analyst: Why?*

> ◗ *Patient: Well, as you say, out of envy.*
> ◗ *Analyst: That is the fundamental question: how to see envy if it is the opposite of awareness. How can we see something that cannot be seen?*

If envy is the act of not seeing, how can the human being see something that cannot be seen, or rather, something that is invisible? To see envy in others is easier, but we are blind to envy in ourselves. If envy is blindness, the moment a person succeeds in seeing it, it will automatically disappear. But this seeing depends upon recognizing envy in oneself; that is, in conscientizing it, which is a mixed process of knowing and feeling.

People are unaware of what they envy because the envy itself renders them unconscious. This is the great human drama: man is a victim of something he does not perceive — in other words, the human being has no consciousness of the very thing that troubles him the most. Modern civilization has essentially been built under the sign of envy.

> ◗ *Analyst: Why do you think you don't want to see your mistakes?*
> ◗ *Patient: Because I don't want to be a bad person, or see what bad attitudes I have.*

Recognizing one's own shortcomings depends upon admitting that envy is at the root of the problem, that it is the cause of all ills. If this were not so, all difficulties would be easily resolved.

Destructive acts are done unconsciously — which is the same as saying that the destructive element is the unconscious. If at the moment we were doing something destructive we became conscious of what we were doing, we would not commit that act. Therefore, we can say that awareness is virtue, which means that it connects the human being to goodness.

The only way to help oneself is by being willing to see one's mistakes; just as the surest way to harm oneself is to be unwilling to see them. It seems as though the human being drives with one foot constantly on the brake, denying the consciousness that leads to goodness, truth and beauty.

10 Lack of awareness is basically envy, which keeps the human being alienated

Lack of awareness and envy are practically one and the same, removing the individual from reality. Similarly, consciousness and reality are also one and the same, acting as a brake against envy. The origin of envy lies in the pleasure of using the senses; and reality follows upon reason and love, which at first glance seem to be sterile elements. We see, then, that man's fundamental problem is one of consciousness, not the unconscious to which Freud and his followers gave such importance. To perceive is first to become aware of one's consciousness so as to then see one's envy, which causes so many problems all through life.

> ▶ *Patient: The world is happy on the eve of the Third Millennium and I am sad and angry.*
> ▶ *Analyst: Is the happiness of others making you green with envy?*
> ▶ *Patient: That's right. Wherever I am I'm always dying of envy.*
> ▶ *Analyst: But the fact that you joke about it like that is a sign that you don't feel your envy — which indicates that you are dominated by it, even when you talk about it.*

We can say that the human being is either conscious, simultaneously perceiving the good and the evil in himself and in the world around him, or he is alienated and has no idea of either the problems or the good that exist. When we perceive good, we also perceive evil. But if we are not conscious of good, we will also be unaware of the evil in force everywhere.

Wherever man goes, he must be conscious of the evil in his actions, thoughts and feelings. It is not consciousness that perceives, but rather perception *is* consciousness, just as envy is not the *cause* of alienation, but rather alienation *is* envy.

> ❱ *Patient: I feel like leaving analysis because I believe I'm getting worse.*
> ❱ *Analyst: Are you worse or are you seeing now that you are worse than you thought?*

When we open ourselves to consciousness, we begin to believe that we were better off being alienated, which means that we confuse seeing with being.

> ❱ *Patient: When they talk about someone in the group psychotherapy session, I note that everything they say is correct. But when they talk about me, I don't believe what they say.*
> ❱ *Analyst: Why do you think you don't accept what the group says about you?*
> ❱ *Patient: Because I don't want to become aware of my problems.*
> ❱ *Analyst: Or because you don't want to stop being envious?*

What I am showing is that our unwillingness to accept seeing our own problems is a way of preserving the pleasure of envy, even though this attitude causes us great harm. Sanity does not result from consciousness, but rather consciousness *is* sanity. Just as only a person with good eyesight can see imperfections, illness is not a consequence of alienation but a denial of the desire to see.

11 We have trouble perceiving our envy because it is a non-feeling

We don't give much thought to envy because it is an anti-emotion, yet we give enormous importance to sex because it involves the senses, and mainly feelings. Because the envious block all that they feel, they believe they're better than others — after all, how could someone who is out of touch with their feelings think they do anything bad? Nevertheless, they are full of bad intentions and simply don't perceive them.

Since envy is a non-feeling, it is as though it does not exist, which means that the greater the envy, the more perfect the person thinks he is! When intellectuals form their societies and academies, they think they are taking part in perfect organizations — which is why the most dangerous ideas sprout from there, unquestioned. There is no doubt that people who show their emotions are much less harmful than those who close themselves off in their intellectual pursuits. The latter become the psychopaths, who appear calm but may suddenly attack and even murder. The conclusion we reach is that those who give magnificent "sermons" and spout moral advice are the most harmful to society, since they have learned to hide all of their short-comings — leading others to do the same. Envy is a synonym for unconsciousness, lack of awareness.

▶ *Patient: I can't play the guitar well because my hand is too small.*

▶ *Analyst: What do you associate your small hand with?*
▶ *Patient: A defect.*
▶ *Analyst: So you see the problem in your hand, not in your attitude of opposing what is good.*

When a lecturer gives a talk, the audience grasps only as much as their envy allows them to perceive. When a person tries to learn, his mind is invaded by all sorts of bad "feelings": not only envy but anger, arrogance, megalomania and malice — attitudes that attack the truth from all sides.

▶ *Patient: All of my husband's success depends on me.*
▶ *Analyst: How so?*
▶ *Patient: It's something spiritual that I can't quite explain.*

It is important to note that it is precisely the least capable people who have an uncommonly superior idea about themselves because they are out of contact with reality and therefore have a delusional idea about life. Because the unconscious is envy and envy is blindness, the human being is generally out of touch with reality. And the more immobilized a person is, the farther from reality is the life he imagines.

▶ *Patient: In the group therapy sessions I keep quiet, just like I did in college and even at home.*
▶ *Analyst: Why do you think you do this?*
▶ *Patient: I think it's because I am very cerebral, very intellectual.*
▶ *Analyst: Isn't it because you reject what is important?*

The envious person appears to be cold, does not participate, and isolates himself — unwilling to feel, or rather, unable to feel — for envy is the denial of love, which is the only true feeling.

Envy causes a person to become paralyzed, devoid of action, because it is an anti-feeling, an opposition to being.

> ⟩ *Patient: When I was in France I read your second book on metaphysics and I became paralyzed to the point of not being able to walk.*
> ⟩ *Analyst: What ideas do you have about the book?*
> ⟩ *Patient: It deals with spiritual influence over the human being, and I thought I was being dominated by spirits.*

Envy paralyzes even our understanding because it annuls the truth. This explains how illness originates from envy due to the enormous contraction it causes to our mental and physical processes.

12 What we call the unconscious is basically envy, the opposite of consciousness

To understand the process of conscientization, it is important to see that consciousness and envy are opposed to one another. To understand reality (what is good, true and aesthetic), a person cannot be very envious, because envy is a process of inversion. Achieving consciousness is basically the same as perceiving envy, because in the face of any knowledge, we enter into contact with envy and its consequences. The fact that we have to make an effort to achieve consciousness is due to the fact that envy blocks consciousness. If it were not for envy we would have total awareness. Basically then, consciousness means becoming aware of envy so that perception can be as complete as possible. I can even go as far as to say that if there were no envy, there would be no need for schools, training and study.

> ▶ *Patient (a woman): I don't like children.*
> ▶ *Analyst : What do you associate children with?*
> ▶ *Patient: They're all little pests.*
> ▶ *Analyst: Or is it that they show you your own "pestiness"?*

After a few moments of silence, I asked:
> ▶ *Analyst: Is that the only thing children remind you of?*
>   *Don't you also think they're beautiful, innocent, happy?*

The Origin Of Illness

- *Patient: I don't have any pleasant ideas about them.*
- *Analyst: Haven't you ever held a child in your lap?*
- *Patient: Never. I would never do that. I can't stand them. I was rejected and that's why I reject them now.*
- *Analyst: I believe you reject children because of the consciousness they bring you.*
- *Patient: It just hasn't worked out for me. When I was I was nine or ten years old I used to like children.*
- *Analyst: I believe that all you have to do is return to the natural feeling of love which you have completely repressed and you will also go back to doing what is right.*

Changing the subject, she said:

- *My boss is two-faced. When I do something wrong, he is extremely demanding, but when another person he likes does the same thing, he has no problem with it. No wonder you yourself said there ought not to be bosses in this world!*

As the reader can see, this patient is opposed to all the good that life has to offer, demonstrating that her extreme envy causes her to become estranged from all the marvelous things life offers for free.

- *Patient: When I wrote this book I had no idea of the problems it would cause me.*
- *Analyst: How so?*
- *Patient: I didn't know that I would have to cite all the sources I used and that the photos I published were copyrighted and I didn't have the right to use them.*
- *Analyst: So what you are saying is that you only listen to your own thoughts and pay no attention to the laws of society.*

A significant characteristic of extremely envious individuals is that they do not pay attention to the laws of society or even to the laws of nature, but rather attempt to create a universe that functions in accordance with their inverted ideas. Unconscious behavior — about which philosophers and scientists such as Descartes, Schelling, Schopenhauer and Nietzsche talked, but to which Freud gave a different meaning, believing that the unconscious was the basis of psychic life — is in fact merely the opposite of conscious behavior. At any rate, people become ill because they fail to follow the ethical guidelines of life and thus think and act in accordance with the envy they feel — thereby inverting all of the rules of normal living.

The unconscious as Freud saw it does not exist. Something that is not, an absence (as the unconscious is referred to) has no existence — nor much less can it be the basis of the human psyche. Freud's theory paved the way for the manifestation of all the delusions of the human mind, as though we were free to be demented.

13 To "know thyself" as Socrates intended depends on our awareness of envy

Willingness to see our errors is essential if we are to follow Socrates' well-known advice of "know thyself,"and above all if we are to correct individual and social pathology. Unconsciousness is synonymous with evil and goodness with consciousness, which is why the sick person has no perception of his errors. In other words, evil is alienation and goodness is knowledge.

As the reader will see, before the intellect functions, there is a series of factors that determine knowing or not; that is, understanding occurs as a consequence of a prior attitude connected to feelings and the will. And the degree to which we accept being ethical also enters here and in turn determines the level of perception we achieve.

There are three fundamental elements (attitudes) that cause illness: the first is obviously envy, which I consider to be the same as the Freudian unconscious; the second is resistance to consciousness or censorship of it, which keep us from seeing the cause of illness; and the third is projection, a consequence of the two prior elements, by which the already sick person attributes all of his destructive attitudes to something or someone in the exterior world. Of the three, censorship is the most active and dangerous for the sick person because it prevents the mind from working with consciousness and overloads the psycho-physical structure.

The Origin Of Illness

Censorship is characterized by unethical behavior.

> ◗ *Patient: I dreamed I was hugging and kissing a disgusting fat woman.*
> ◗ *Analyst: What do you associate that woman with?*
> ◗ *Patient: Bad habits, things in the past.*
> ◗ *Analyst: The dream makes you aware of how attached you are to your pathology, to your bad habits — showing how unwilling you are to change your behavior.*

The attitude of this patient illustrates two factors: first, the desire to persist in pathological behavior (because it brings pleasure); and second, how horrible it is to persist in destructive behavior, which debases the person.

First comes envy, then censorship of it; and if the censorship is very strong, the person will project his problems onto others. Practically speaking, censorship follows envy and to the same degree: the greater a person's censorship, the stronger their envy — and the greater their projection.

> ◗ *Patient: I dreamed I saw PJ fall on the ground and JP censoring his attitude.*
> ◗ *Analyst: What do you associate the attitudes of PJ and JP with?*
> ◗ *Patient: The former with malice and the latter with censorship.*

As we can see from this example, malice and censorship occur on the same level — which makes it possible to say that the process of censorship is the most pernicious of all.

Knowledge comes as a result of consciousness, which is a prior combination of intellect and feeling. But in order to gain awareness, we must accept seeing ourselves as we are, defects and all — except that in this case, this "acceptance" only occurs if we are also willing to correct our shortcomings. Note that our inner, psychological life is extremely intricate, with one element linked to the other and all elements interconnected like an enormous web. And like a web, it can break apart or not function well if any one of the elements is missing or defective.

14 We tend to disparage the good we receive

▶ *Patient: I became very angry with my dentist because she told me I had a problem with my teeth that I didn't have.*
▶ *Analyst: In general, has her treatment been positive or negative?*
▶ *Patient: Ninety-percent positive, but I can't seem to forget her incorrect diagnosis.*

This example illustrates how we generally reject the good we receive, giving any shabby excuse we can find to demean it. My point of view here is unique, opposite to most other orientations, which is why many who read my work may find it unusual.

The profession of psychoanalyst is the most difficult of all, because analysts must deal with the enmity of their patients, of their colleagues in other medical professions (who treat patients organically with medication), and of society itself, which justifies its "feelings" of envy any way it can. In other words, the true treatment would be to cure envy, which few people are able to control — but when psychoanalytical treatment is effective, it is attacked precisely because it works to eliminate envious "feelings."

Because of envy, the human being negates the greatness for which he was created and belittles the genius of those who accept goodness. Envy causes us to turn against others and at the same time turn others against us.

> *Patient: I have a student who doesn't like the texts I read in class.*
> *Analyst: What do you think of this student?*
> *Patient: She is very envious and aggressive. In fact, her boss told her she makes a lot of enemies at work because of her antagonistic attitude.*

The point made by this example is very important, because it illustrates how envy leads us to reject what is best and causes others to reject us as well when they see we don't follow what is most worthy and therefore have nothing very useful to contribute. Thus, the envious are the most likely to be scorned by society while most of the time remaining oblivious to how others feel about them.

Patient JP said he did not want to do what his family advised him to do.

> *Analyst: What do you see in your family?*
> *Patient: I see a lot of value in my parents, who worked hard to become reasonably well off. But I want to have my own independent life.*
> *Analyst: So what you are saying is that you don't accept your family's advice because you are envious of their success.*

To gain wisdom and understanding, we must follow the valuable guidance of the great thinkers and talented people who came before us. How can anyone truly understand any guidance, correct philosophy or the right way to do something if they strongly reject goodness?

> *Patient: This week I was very nervous.*

- *Analyst: About what?*
- *Patient: Well, initially about the lecture I had to give, but it turned out fine.*
- *Analyst: So, you're saying that when things are fine you get nervous?*
- *Patient: Later I also became worried about my son's cold.*
- *Analyst What do you associate his cold with?*
- *Patient: Illness, feeling bad.*
- *Analyst: But in general isn't he healthy?*
- *Patient: Yes.*
- *Analyst: Then why do you keep thinking about his illness, especially when it's nothing serious?*

It is very common for envious people to spend all of their time thinking about problems and difficulties instead of being grateful and happy for what they have. Unhappy people are those who put themselves above others and expect to be served — while happy people are humble, believing they receive more than enough from life.

15 Personal success depends on acceptance of the success of others

In order to succeed, one has to accept the success of others. In other words, just as the past must inevitably be a part of the present and even the future must be incorporated in the present, personal success depends entirely upon one's acceptance of other people's success. Everything we do is interrelated with the accomplishments of others. Therefore, if we admire individuals who are capable and talented, we will automatically emulate them — and in this way do even more than they have done. But if we envy them, we deny and destroy what they accomplished, hold ourselves back, and keep ourselves from achieving success.

Our happiness and well-being depend upon the happiness and well-being of others. When theologians say that one must be charitable to please God, they are referring in the psychological sense to an attitude that is fundamental for happiness. Personal good only comes as a result of the good others enjoy.

> ▶ *Patient: (crying) This year I tried really hard to do well in my work and now at the end of the year I've ruined everything with my attitude.*
> ▶ *Analyst: Why are you sobbing?*
> ▶ *Patient: I don't exactly know.*

> *Analyst: It's because you want to keep on behaving destructively and your co-workers won't let you. You felt bad because you regretted having done good, so you found a way to ruin things.*

In fact, the reason most people accept the pathological behavior of their leaders is because those leaders openly do the harmful things that a large part of the population would like to do.

> *Patient: I can't seem to accept what's good. When JFK Jr. died, I cried because it reminded me of all the people who are against the Kennedy family.*
> *Analyst: What do you associate that family with?*
> *Patient: With the only rich family in the United States that's good.*
> *Analyst: In this case you identify with those who attack that family.*
> *Patient: Yes, I think so. In a way, I don't think good things have a chance, especially in my country, the United States.*
> *Analyst: You're saying that you don't give good things a chance to exist in your life. On the other hand, it is precisely this admiration you have for the Kennedy family that gives you equilibrium.*

This is the great dilemma of envy, for one can clearly see the problem of envy in others but we are blind to the problem in ourselves.

1. To be effective, psychotherapy must work with the consciousness of envy.

2. Envy is the denial of awareness; the wish not to exist; man's original sin.

3. Envy is the universal cause of all problems; the root of all suffering.

4. There is a demonic quality to the inward manifestation of envy; it makes life hell.

5. What harms the human being and humanity most is envy. If the human race does not perceive envy, it will perish; but if we become aware of envy we can return to paradise. Consciousness of envy is mankind's salvation.

6. If we didn't have envy our success would be limitless.

7. What Freud called the unconscious is basically synonymous with envy.

8. Envy makes the personality extremely rigid.

9. The primary purpose of consciousness is to perceive envy.

10. Envy can be measured by how unconscious a person is.

11. Envy is saying "no" to goodness, choosing the ugly over the beautiful and lies instead of truth.

12. Man generally despises the good he receives.

Part 2

CENSORSHIP

Our fundamental human problem lies in our censorship of any consciousness of envy – which is why psychotherapy is the process that can break down our resistance toward seeing our bad "feelings" and destructive attitudes.

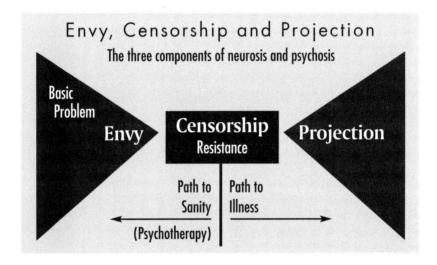

Envy, Censorship and Projection

The three components of neurosis and psychosis

Basic Problem

Envy

Censorship
Resistance

Projection

Path to Sanity | Path to Illness

(Psychotherapy)

1 Envy blocks our consciousness and keeps us blinded

Most manifestations of envy require an act of faith more than actual perception to be treated, for how can something that is imperceptible be perceived? And this is true not just for envy but for all the other attitudes that the religious called the deadly sins: pride, anger, sloth (laziness), gluttony, avarice (greed) and lust. Only that person who embraces goodness (good thoughts, feelings and actions) is conscious of evil (the denial of goodness), because goodness favors perception — while a person who adopts pathological attitudes (errors) remains outside of consciousness, unseeing.

> ▶ *Patient (a doctor): I admit that I am envious of you because of the innovative work you have done in the area of psychosomatic medicine.*
> ▶ *Analyst: In other words you are opposed to psychosomatic medicine.*
> ▶ *Patient: I don't think I'm actually opposed to it, but I'm trying to add something to this field, to understand it really well.*
> ▶ *Analyst: Because of the way envy works, you don't see that you're opposed to your own profession.*

Because envy is a repression of consciousness, it is very difficult to perceive. When all is said and done, envy is a very shameful attitude that seeks to destroy the good of others while also destroying one's own good — which shows how stupid we humans can really be.

> ▶ *Patient: I got furious when you told me my article was riddled with errors. Even Jose de Alencar and Machado de Assis [renowned Brazilian authors] made mistakes!*
> ▶ *Analyst: What does the perception of those mistakes in your writing signify?*

The patient did not answer, so I continued.

> ▶ *Analyst: Could it mean a correction of your defects, which is something you don't want to do?*
> ▶ *Patient: That makes sense!*
> ▶ *Analyst: Then this shows that you always want to make mistakes, and you become furious when someone keeps you from doing it - - precisely because you think there is some advantage in being wrong.*

The unconscious, as the word itself implies, cannot exist in and of itself except as a denial of consciousness, which truly exists. Therefore, we can say that envy is a negation of consciousness because it is the anti-sentiment par excellence; or better, the denial of affection.

Good acts sharpen our awareness; evil acts dull our awareness. In other words, it is our desire to do good that brings us consciousness, and our denial of goodness that negates consciousness. Therefore, we can say that the affectionate person is conscious, while the angry, aggressive person is devoid of consciousness.

When we turn to our delirious fantasies, we fall into unreality because we lose contact with the real world. Our inner life is nourished by our relationship with reality, which provides all the riches our inner life needs to exist. To like or love is to establish contact with the real world; to dislike is to remain addicted to our egoism: our deliriums.

It is important to understand that true contact with both the outside world and inner life depends on the degree of envy the person has. When one's envy is very great, it is difficult for us to perceive reality — and everything we do, inwardly or outwardly, will be riddled with error. Therefore, contact with reality (inside and outside ourselves) will depend on our having a lesser degree of envy.

2 The main characteristic of illness is lack of awareness

The main characteristic of illness is the absence of awareness, for the person who has harmful attitudes does not perceive what he is doing. Only the person whose attitudes and actions are good is conscious of the harm he causes. Thus, we can say that illness is unconsciousness, lack of awareness; or better, unconsciousness is illness.

> *Patient: My husband doesn't allow me to move anything in our home. If I move the table even slightly he puts it back in its original place.*
> *Analyst: What do you associate your husband's attitude with?*
> *Patient: Not wanting any change for the better.*
> *Analyst: Not accepting the perception of a rigid, sick attitude.*

Whether in its healthy or pathological aspect, we have difficulty seeing life the way it really is — and mainly the goodness life has to offer.

> *Patient: Yesterday I became irritated with my husband. He didn't make the deliveries for our business with the excuse that he didn't have time. But even worse, he is always criticizing me.*

> ❯ *Analyst: Your husband's inactivity shows how he sabotages the business and your censorship of his attitude shows your sabotage.*
> ❯ *Patient: I don't see that attitude in myself, even though my family is incredibly censoring. What I don't like to see is how I'm constantly being reprimanded.*
> ❯ *Analyst: Then at this moment are you censoring your perception?*

Censorship is a Gordian knot in the life of the human being because first, it prevents us from seeing our problems; and second, if we're unaware, how can we become aware of our unawareness? This is why it is necessary to enlist the help of a trained psychoanalyst. As the saying goes: no one can be his own judge and jury.

When patients go into explanations it is because they are censoring, afraid to see what is really going on in their life.

> ❯ *Patient: It seems to be an irreversible process, but the newcomers in our company don't know how to do their work well, and because of this they can't form true relationships... etc. There was a noise in the building where I live. I mentioned it to the doorman and to the building superintendent, but they did nothing about it. I insisted, and then they discovered the noise was a key that kept banging against a door.*
> ❯ *Analyst: What do you associate that noise with in the psychological sense?*
> ❯ *Patient: It reminds me of the secretary who's going to retire and of George, who's very dominating. I also have a problem with premature ejaculation and impotence so its hard to have a girlfriend, but a call girl easily deals with it in other ways such as masturbation.*
> ❯ *Analyst: You see sex as if it were a nightmare, a torment.*

▶ *Patient: Yes, if the problem is impotence I think it's really bad because I'm not gay and I'm not perverted. So the women ask: "Do you have a problem with me?"*
▶ *Analyst: You need to see that the problem of sexual impotence is mainly psychological.*
▶ *Patient: I can still have sex once a week.*
▶ *Analyst: Then, doesn't it seem as if the problem is mostly in your imagination?*

As the reader can see, this person has neither perception of the good things he possesses nor is he aware of his problems.

▶ *Patient: I'm angry about the place I work because the people are low class. I can't get along with any of them.*
▶ *Analyst: Don't you admit that there is a lower class inside yourself?*
▶ *Patient: Oh! Yes, I admit it. But I don't live like I'm low class.*
▶ *Analyst: Does this consciousness make you suffer?*
▶ *Patient: I think I'm getting sick again!*
▶ *Analyst: Illness doesn't exist in and of itself. What exists is the attitude of denying truth and goodness— which we call illness.*
▶ *Patient: Then is "illness" something the human being invented to avoid consciousness?*

As we can see, any illness demonstrates how we close our eyes to consciousness. It follows then that being unconscious and being sick are one and the same.

3 Illness lies in our resistance to consciousness

We become ill because we resist seeing our problems; that is, we constantly attempt to ignore our weak points. As for our qualities, there is no need to focus on them because they form the structure of the personality and of life itself; or better, they exist on their own.

> Patient: I'm so terrified of seeing problems, and as a result I'm unable to show my students their difficulties.
> Analyst: Can you give an example?
> Patient: I'm afraid of seeing any problem, no matter how simple.

If you observe the world around you, you will see that society generally deals only with the positive aspects of the human being — as if there were something wrong with seeing mistakes.

> Patient: I feel like I'm an outsider. I'm afraid of socializing like other people and I can't manage to get over it.
> Analyst: It's important for you to perceive that you live like an outsider.

The Origin Of Illness

▶ *Patient: I've known this for quite some time but I can't manage to change, not even one iota. In fact, my wife always gets very upset about this!*

I include this excerpt from a session of analysis to clarify the fact that since knowledge is an integral part of the being, true understanding of a problem comes only through its correction. This explains the need to know the truth in order to feel well. Practically speaking, love, reality and correct action are what constitute being.

If illness stems mainly from censorship, we are forced to admit that illness is a psychological process that is largely dependent upon the will. This distinction I make is the principal key to resolving the problem of the psychological and sociological pathology of humanity. I believe that our lack of consciousness results from our resistance in seeing our mistakes. It seems that we have no choice: either we accept consciousness and admit goodness into our lives, or we refuse consciousness and disrupt our lives.

4 Neurosis is an attitude of resisting consciousness

Man's inglorious struggle, which Freud called resistance, is a struggle against the consciousness of error. There is no one who does not abhor seeing his mistakes.

> *Patient: I have a real phobia about looking at myself and seeing my mistakes.*
> *Analyst: That's humanity's greatest problem.*
> *Patient: It seems that none of us wants to see the things we do wrong.*

If we consider consciousness in the true sense of the word as being aware of good and evil, we see that it opens a whole new world in all areas of life; whereas the gentler hypotheses (mainly those of Freud, Adler and Klein, which for the most part link consciousness to sexual problems, inferiority complexes and envy of the mother) prevent any deeper understanding of life.

After twenty minutes of silence, I asked the patient:

> *Analyst: Are you meditating today?*
> *Patient: I'm very upset because my new book has too many pages.*

The Origin Of Illness

> ▶ *Analyst: What do you associate that with?*
> ▶ *Patient: My mistake.*

As the reader can see, the patient's anxiety in seeing any flaw in himself demonstrates his weak character. I believe our greatest sin is our attitude of not wanting to see our "sins," our faults. The only way we can expand our knowledge of life and contact genuine reality is by taking a more humble attitude.

> ▶ *Patient: I'm eternally frustrated.*
> ▶ *Analyst: Isn't so much frustration an odd thing? Your attitude shows how you live according to your whims and you feel frustrated because you cannot carry them out.*

The point I wish to make is that the dissatisfied person is that way because he wants to satisfy his every desire, no matter how childish. In fact, this attitude is typical of the infantile personality, interested mainly in getting their own way. The disadvantage of resisting the consciousness of error is that our psychological life remains superficial, preventing us from taking part in the greatness of the universe.

One becomes adult by being aware of one's mistakes, which leads us to greater knowledge. Life is one pathological attitude after another, from start to finish, and yet many people are taken aback when they note anything wrong in themselves or even in society. Nevertheless, only those who are willing to perceive their sick attitudes can succeed in living in accordance with reality.

There is no doubt whatsoever that our life is ruled in great part by our unconscious, of which we have practically no awareness. This discovery of Freud's is the greatest milestone of modern times — and it must be taken into consideration if we wish to understand ourselves and our society.

> *Patient: I dreamed I was with my mother and father traveling on a boat, feeling marvelous. However, my mother argued with my father the entire time.*
> *Analyst: What ideas do you have of your parents?*
> *Patient: My father, young and wonderful; my mother, young and beautiful. Could it be that I wanted my father for myself, as in Freud's Oedipus complex?*
> *Analyst: Or did you envy their happiness and want to destroy it? The Freudian theory (of the Oedipus complex) spread around the world and has kept us from becoming aware of the true cause of problems.*
> *Patient: I had some idea of that but I couldn't admit it before. In fact, in real life my mother was always fighting with my father, making him a victim and provoking him to the point that he would lose control.*
> *Analyst: Why do you think she did that ?*
> *Patient: I think she was envious of my father.*
> *Analyst: An attitude you imitate with your husband?*

Note that by going beyond a Freudian interpretation, patients are led toward a broader view of a better world and begin to see how to deal with all aspects of their lives — not merely a narrow-minded view, which has caused psychiatrists and psychoanalysts in the United States to be referred to as "shrinks."

The human condition can be summed up this way: in order to gain knowledge, we must conscientize our mistakes; that is, become aware of them; but because we have enormous resistance to seeing them, we curtail our knowledge and fall into a state of non-being. This is our pathology.

5 We think consciousness (the perception of problems) is dangerous

> ▶ *Patient: At work I didn't apply for a promotion because I was afraid I wouldn't get it.*
> ▶ *Analyst: Your idea is that if you see your defects you will harm your life. However, it's fundamental to become aware of them so you can know what's best for you.*

Psychological and organic (physical) symptoms are really a type of "perception" that arises to prod us to pay attention to what is happening in our life. And yet, incredible as it may seem, a veritable arsenal of medicines and hospital procedures have been created precisely to hide what these physical and psychological symptoms are trying to reveal. As a result, consciousness — the most important element in life — is eliminated.

If people consider consciousness to be the most dangerous element in their lives, how can we get them to accept it? We need to provide not only psychoanalysis, but also reading material and other information that will help them become aware of this error.

> ▶ *Patient: I dreamed I was going on a trip and at the airport the guard examined my passport very carefully. There was a cat with me that had lost its paw because I wasn't paying attention.*

- *Analyst: What do you associate the guard's attitude and the cat with?*
- *Patient: Lack of attention to what's happening.*
- *Analyst (insisting): And the attitude of the guard?*
- *Patient: A lot of censorship.*
- *Analyst: Or rather, how you keep yourself from seeing the harm in your life precisely because you do not want to see your faults — symbolized by the cat's missing paw.*

The fewer the problems a person sees, the more neurotic that person is; whereas the healthy individual has an acute perception of difficulties because he has less resistance to consciousness.

- *Patient: It seems that after six months of analysis I'm a lot worse!*
- *Analyst: What makes you think that?*
- *Patient: Because when I started my treatment I didn't notice even ten percent of the problems I see now.*
- *Analyst: As your blindness, which is your censorship of consciousness, diminishes, you are able to see your shortcomings more easily.*

To live in reality, we need a certain amount of humility to take us out of our megalomanic delusions. But with arrogance, there is so much fantasy that others cannot establish a relationship with that person. They avoid him, never knowing when he will suddenly become aggressive without any plausible reason.

- *Patient: I dreamed that the ocean waves rose up to my apartment on the twentieth floor, but the only thing I could think about was the harm the waves were doing to my car which was parked down below.*

> *Analyst: What do you associate the waves and the car with?*
> *Patient: The waves with consciousness and car with development and security.*
> *Analyst: In this case you believe that consciousness destroys your development and security.*
> *Patient: In the dream I also saw my mother next to me. She was very calm about what was happening.*
> *Analyst: What do you see in her attitude?*
> *Patient: A person who is unaffected by what is going on around her. I admired her attitude.*
> *Analyst: You admire alienation and want to remain unaffected by what happens.*

We see here that while the patient felt that consciousness (the waves) was dangerous to his development and security, he had no regret when the waves rose up to the twentieth floor. In any event, the patient's thinking was inverted in associating his success with the car and not with his apartment, which withstood the rising waters!

Traditional psychoanalysis believes that we become sick because of an inner universe that Freud called the unconscious, and that as long as the unconscious remains unconscious, there can be neither cure nor progress. I believe the opposite: we become ill precisely because we do not accept consciousness — which also brings us awareness of wrong attitudes and problems. We have therefore created tremendous opposition to wisdom and understanding, with the result that human beings and the society they have built have become sick and riddled with flaws because of faults they are unwilling to see. I can say without a shadow of a doubt that pathology, illness, is the attitude of opposing consciousness.

Unwillingness to become aware of problems is an attitude that causes damage to the individual and to society, making both vulnerable to the problems they do not want to see. This explains why so many people resist psychotherapy: it stirs up everything that people and society have so carefully tried to hide.

6 The Freudian unconscious should be referred to as censorship

There is no such thing as an unconscious impulse. What exists instead is really censorship, whose role is to oppose consciousness. There is feeling — which is positive when it is love (the only true feeling), or which can be negative when it is replaced by envy, hatred, bitterness, slander and other destructive attitudes.

On the other hand, the way to tell how loving a person is is to observe how conscious the person is. That is why the great 5th century thinker Saint Augustine said "love and do as you wish," for when we act out of love, we forgo any sort of negativity. As incredible as it may seem, we would have to convince ourselves that the greatest discovery of the 19th century — the unconscious, which seemed to have revolutionized all other concepts, was nothing but a huge bluff if the unconscious is seen as an entity within the human psyche.

Tom Jobim, renowned Brazilian jazz musician, once said that it was a crime to be successful in Brazil, but actually this is so in any country. Those who accomplish great things come under attack from their own family, then from close associates and even from the government of their country. I propose that envy dominates the lives of individuals and nations, blocking their development. It follows then that we human beings are capable of achieving success only if our envy is not too great.

> *Patient: My aunt took a turn for the worse and I had to put her in the hospital. I feel totally lost and don't know what to make of what the doctor said.*
> *Analyst: What do you associate your aunt's hospitalization with?*
> *Patient: Death.*
> *Analyst: It seems as though you are very attached to matters of illness, death and problems. Your biggest concern is with negative things and you pay little attention to what is positive — which is what is truly important in life.*

In general, because consciousness is light and knowledge, those who have few ideals also fail to develop it. Because of their strong censorship, they prevent consciousness from existing in their inner self.

> *Patient: I dreamed I was cleaning a room.*
> *Analyst: What does cleaning mean to you?*
> *Patient: It means to leave everything clean.*
> *Analyst: And in the psychological sense, what does it represent?*

Since the patient did not know how to respond, I said:
> *Analyst: Couldn't it be showing you that you need to clean what is "dirty" so you can see the good, beautiful and truthful reality beneath it?*

As we can see in this excerpt from a session of analysis, the greater the censorship, the less awareness there is of the wonders of the universe — precisely because of the envy (which the patient identified with dirt in the dream) there is toward everything that is magnificent.

7 Our greatest problem is thinking that what we don't see won't hurt us

What is our greatest problem? Believing that we are unaffected by what we do not see. We think, for example, that if we unconsciously do something harmful or unconsciously harbor negative "feelings," we won't suffer the consequences. But our behavior speaks for itself, producing positive or negative results whether we were aware at the time or not. Most people think that if they ignore their bad ideas, emotions and attitudes, they will be free of them. In fact, it is this attitude that has led the world to its present disastrous state.

In other words, we are responsible for what we do not know, which is the same as saying that we are responsible for our "ignorance," because in one's inner self there exists a commandment to do good and avoid evil. If we ignore the latter, we are doubly guilty: first, for not knowing what we ought to know; and second, especially, for choosing ignorance, the source of the worst pathology. The main question is: if someone is doing something wrong and isn't aware of it, will that person be harmed or not? Yet how can we blame a person for doing something wrong if they are unaware of what they were doing? First of all, we have to question whether the person really did not know what he was doing; and second, whether the consequences of his wrong-doing are connected in any way to that knowledge or not.

> *Patient: I dreamt that two men came into my house and suddenly became dangerous.*
> *Analyst: What do you associate those men with?*
> *Patient: They seemed inoffensive but they were threatening.*

The patient then added that she wasn't feeling well but believed everything was going along well in her life.

We note here in the dream, because censorship is diminished during sleep, she was fully aware of something dangerous in her inner self — and was doing everything she could to avoid seeing it during her waking hours. We also have to consider the fact that many of us oppose knowledge because we have a preconceived notion about it, as though we were not obliged to know. In this case, there enters the commonly-held belief in society that awareness is not always beneficial.

We believe that if we do not see something, we are not responsible for it; or better, that we have no part in it. This is why we try to ignore things as much as possible — to diminish everything we can in our lives. The envious person values mediocre individuals and devalues those who are truly worthy. Generally speaking, this is mankind's greatest inversion, systematically destroying its geniuses and saints while encouraging the wrongdoers and the incapable.

> *Patient: When I appear on TV, I'm nervous the entire time and make lots of mistakes.*
> *Analyst: Why do you think that happens?*
> *Patient: It's because I want to appear well-balanced — yet I know that in reality I don't make an effort to become better.*
> *Analyst: Then isn't it that when you speak on TV you*

are forced to see the imperfections you don't believe you have?

This is also why the very envious are opposed to work, because that is where they demonstrate all of their incompetence.

Envy lies at the root of all problems and vices in the individual and in society. In order to know if a person is honorable and admirable or dishonorable and unexceptional, one need only verify how envious the person is. What I wish to make clear is that envy is the cause of all problems, the root of all evil, leading us to be totally incongruous, totally out of sync.

The Origin Of Illness

8 It is extremely dishonest to think that all harmful acts are committed unconsciously

The most dishonest thing we can do is say that we make our mistakes unconsciously. If we were not dishonest in this way, there would be no illness, decadence or death.

▶ *Patient: By realizing I'm responsible for what happened in my life, I see that I've ruined it quite a bit. Of course it would have to be this way because if people hide from themselves what they know, they also forfeit their awareness.*

▶ *Analyst: And your biggest dishonesty is not admitting that you yourself do this.*

▶ *Patient: I don't know…it seems that after awhile a person is no longer aware of what he is doing!*

▶ *Analyst: Yes, it seems that after awhile a person's consciousness becomes "calloused," making it useless. But even so, a small voice always remains, warning us to do good and avoid evil.*

No one becomes ill without a reason, because illness is a type of violence committed against one's nature, preventing it from developing as it should.

▶ *Patient: I was giving English lessons to two secretaries who work in an import-export firm. They said they had to lie about the price of the product so the company could have greater profit. I told them that if they continued to be dishonest like that they would get sick. Right after that, they stopped coming to class.*

❱ *Analyst: Why do you think that happened?*

❱ *Patient: They didn't want to see their dishonesty.*

❱ *Analyst: No, I'm asking about your attitude!*

❱ *Patient: Maybe I was too harsh with them.*

❱ *Analyst: Don't you see your envy here? If their job was to generate profit for their company by charging the highest price they could, they would be fired if they didn't do that.*

❱ *Patient: But isn't that dishonest?*

❱ *Analyst: Or is it that you became envious of the money they made in their work and did everything you could to keep them from continuing.*

Note that because the patient could not see his own dishonesty, he gave the secretaries advice that would have lowered the company's profits. The whole purpose of sales is to sell something for more than you paid for it. In any case, because the patient did not perceive his envy, the advice he gave the young women was inverted, opposite to what it should have been.

Being willing to see one's envy is being willing to see one's own indignity. Patient FA remarked that he was having physical symptoms that revealed his unsuitable behavior.

❱ *Patient: It is very humbling to admit that I am sick as a result of dishonesty.*

❱ *Analyst: That realization is crucial for your cure.*

This excerpt from a session of analysis serves to emphasize

the need for humility if we are to get in touch with ourselves. We human beings have chosen destructive attitudes for our lives but are unwilling to recognize them — which is yet another destructive attitude, because without awareness there is no possibility of correcting them even if we might wish to!

I have shown over and over again that most of what Freud referred to as the unconscious is nothing more, nothing less than the effort we make to hide the envy we feel. Obviously this "feeling" is too shameful to be admitted normally, so we are led to try to forget it any way we can. The result is that by ignoring envy, it continues to exist and its negative force becomes even greater.

> ▶ *Patient: GG won't let me play in the concert he's planning.*
> ▶ *Analyst: Have you asked him why not?*
> ▶ *Patient: No.*
> ▶ *Analyst: What he told me was that you saw how successful his last presentation was and so now you want to play out of envy just to ruin his work. He plays classical music and you play only pop music, and you hardly practice at all!*
> ▶ *Patient: In this case, it does seem to be envy.*
> ▶ *Analyst: The question is that everything you do in your life is motivated by this desire to destroy and to oppose goodness, and because of your censorship you don't want to become conscious of it.*

The Freudian idea that the human being is completely at the mercy of his unconscious is the greatest deception of the twentieth century because it makes a person even sicker. On the other hand, the new way of looking at the unconscious has the potential to completely revolutionize the world in the years to come.

9 We bear greater responsibility for what we ignore than for what we know

We bear much greater responsibility for what we "don't know" than for what we are willing to know. At first glance, this paradoxical idea seems to be a mistake. And yet, if we analyze the consequences civilization has reaped by believing otherwise, we are forced to admit that we have arrived at an impasse which can be resolved only by accepting such responsibility. To begin with, we need to look back at Plato's heuristic theory of knowledge and logic: no one tries to know what he already knows nor much less does he try to know what he doesn't know, because no one tries to become aware of what he is already aware of nor much less does he try to become aware of what he does not know exists.

In the field of psychopathology, the idea that we are not responsible for what we don't know has served as a pretext to excuse people from being accountable for even the most senseless acts.

> ▶ *Patient: Ever since I was a child I have cried without knowing why — and I now see it was out of pure envy. Once, instead of going to sleep on the bed where my mother could see me, I lay on the floor just to irritate her. Later, I always saw myself as a victim of others in an attempt to ignore any guilt of my own.*

Many criminal lawyers use the idea of "unconscious impulses" as a defense in an attempt to ignore the fact that a whole time of preparation is necessary beforehand to plan the details of a crime. So we see that the idea of "not knowing" is not exactly that — even though at the moment of the offense the perpetrator may not have been fully conscious of what he was doing.

We humans have invented the idea that it's possible to hide our bad intentions and, worse yet, that for the most part we will not have to suffer the consequences of what we do wrong. The purpose of psychotherapy is to work with the malice, the bad intentions of the person who has learned to hide his erroneous thoughts. In general, when we say that a person does not know, it would be more accurate to say that they don't *want* to know.

In regard to Plato's heuristic principle, his doctrine of reminiscence or recollection, I would like to clarify that knowing is not exactly remembering (as he believed, from the world of ideas), but rather a reawakening of something that already exists in ourselves — for we cannot comprehend anything outside of ourselves unless there is a corresponding reference point within us. In general, people are only aware of those things that interest them, otherwise they will say they know nothing about the matter.

Consciousness is with us from birth. In order to deal with our psychopathology, we must see how much and why we reject a good deal of what our consciousness shows us. Furthermore, I believe that censorship is our greatest impediment to it. In short, we are conscious of what we feel, think and do. I am not saying that we should be responsible for knowing what is happening on distant planets, but we are responsible for knowing what is going on inside ourselves. However, we make an enormous effort to ignore what we know — and this is our greatest mistake.

▶ *Patient: I don't feel good today.*
▶ *Analyst: Are you ill?*
▶ *Patient: No, I just don't feel good.*
▶ *Analyst: But if you were doing something useful you wouldn't have time to think about your 'cadaver,' as they say in Vienna.*

This example illustrates how, when a person does not do the good he ought to do, he creates very strong feelings of guilt which he may not always perceive but which will affect him nevertheless.

Freud's attempt to view psychological life in a scientific way was very naïve since he violated most of the standards of logic and coherence. First, he proposed that a negative element (the unconscious) could bring enlightenment to mankind. Second, he proposed that illness stemmed from that same element. Third, and worst of all, from the start he devalued consciousness — the element that in every sense is the most important in life!

10 We take our pathological attitudes with us everywhere we go

Religious fanatics generally believe that we human beings are sometimes led by demons to do evil things — not that our behavior is routinely linked to evil.

> ◗ *Patient: SM sometimes acts as if he is possessed.*
> ◗ *Analyst: Sometimes or always?*

The patient's idea here is completely wrong. It illustrates how we incorrectly believe that the framework of our society and the way we behave are basically correct and that we only occasionally stray from the proper path — instead of seeing that all of our paths tend to be pathological. Nor could it be otherwise, since sickness predominates in humankind and in society.

This being the case, we must always be suspicious of any attitude we take, because all of them contain some harmful element. In fact, no human act is entirely free of error. The following are but a few examples among all the rest.

> ◗ When the crusades of the Middle Ages were launched to liberate Jerusalem from the infidels, the true intention was to fortify ecclesiastical power which was in crisis at the time;

❱ When the United States attacked Iran after the invasion of Kuwait, the true intention was to fortify the U.S. military-industrial complex — not to mention the fact that the area was an enormous profit center for American drug traffickers;

❱ When Clinton denounced child labor in Brazil, his comments seemed noble, but in reality he was trying to keep Brazil from competing in the international shoe market — and even worse, it meant taking food off the tables of the poor families those minors helped support.

❱ *Patient: I always make the same mistakes.*
❱ *Analyst: And how does realizing this now make you feel?*
❱ *Patient: Much calmer than in the past because I think now I'm able to correct the worst ones.*

I would like to make it clear that the purpose of psychotherapy is not to "eliminate" problems but rather to make the patient aware of them — although the worst mistakes are also corrected as a result. In fact, the only possible way to correct any difficulty is by knowing its cause.

❱ *Patient: I'm not able to get over my sicknesses.*
❱ *Analyst: Your problem is that you aren't willing to face your problems.*
❱ *Patient: But I suffer because of my depression.*
❱ *Analyst: No, you suffer because you don't want to see the cause of the depression.*
❱ *Patient: But I also have pains in my body.*
❱ *Analyst: Everyone suffers pain because of their behavior. Why should you be any different?*

The highly neurotic person expects the process of analysis to eliminate his problems, the same way a surgeon closes an ulcer or removes tonsils, an appendix or a tumor — a process which is contrary to what it should be, because it hides the real cause of illness, which is psychological.

The basic purpose of psychotherapy is to not to "eliminate" problems but to become aware of them in order to deal with them. What happens is that we want to resolve our conflicts miraculously without having to get to the root of them — the same attitude we have always had in all areas and eras. One example is modern medicine, which is like medieval alchemy in its attempt to cure mental and physical illness with magic potions.

> ❱ *Patient: I don't talk about my daughter's problems in group therapy because I'm afraid of being attacked.*
> ❱ *Analyst: What do you associate group therapy with?*
> ❱ *Patient: With help.*
> ❱ *Analyst: Then you see help as an attack, goodness as something evil.*

Our greatest problem is not that we have problems but that we don't want to see them. From the moment of birth to the end of our life on earth we must confront hundreds of difficulties every day, which can be worked with only if we are willing to accept consciousness of them.

11 Symptoms are necessary for awareness

Mankind has always considered psychological symptoms to be highly dangerous for those who suffer them. I propose that if we did not have those signs of our psychopathology, it would be impossible to treat any type of mental illness.

> ▶ *Patient: I am very fearful now that I have stopped taking my medication.*
> ▶ *Analyst: Now that you have stopped taking your medication, you are more aware of your fear.*
> ▶ *Patient: I would like to control this fear. My hands and feet are ice cold.*
> ▶ *Analyst: Without a doubt you are getting better because you are becoming aware of how you feel.*
> ▶ *Patient: Yes, it seems as if the medication masks what I feel.*
> ▶ *Analyst: What's important is always to be aware of your feelings — even feelings of panic — if you are to avoid the risk of a heart attack or some other serious physical problem.*
> ▶ *Patient: But what can I do not to feel so much?*
> ▶ *Analyst: Your best defense is precisely to be aware of what you feel.*

The Origin Of Illness

For us to become aware of any physical illness there must be some symptom (pain, discomfort) in that organ so that the physician can treat it. In psychological life the process is exactly the same: anxiety, depression, phobia, mania, a persecution complex and such serve the same purpose.

> ▶ *Patient: I used to get bad attacks of the hiccups, which have returned now. And yet during the time I didn't have them, I had no perception whatsoever. It seems we only have contact with what is bad!*
> ▶ *Analyst: If it were not for that symptom, you would have no idea that there was something behind the hiccups that you should know about.*

Typically, whenever we become ill, we run to the pharmacy to free ourselves of the problem by taking medicine — and in the process lose contact with an awareness that is fundamental for our existence.

> ▶ *Analyst: You're very quiet today.*
> ▶ *Patient: I never know what to say. I've been very nervous lately.*
> ▶ *Analyst: Or do you now see that you're nervous, which is a very important perception?*
> ▶ *Patient: I've been this way since I became involved with spiritism, which has taught me to have love, to trust in God — but I see that I don't trust Him the way I would like to.*
> ▶ *Analyst: Do you now see that you don't trust in God as much as you thought you did, and that not accepting this perception makes you very nervous?*

Consciousness is perception, whether of good or of evil — for awareness of evil is always enormously beneficial.

12 Consciousness is health; alienation is illness

Envy (pathology) is not perceived because it is a denial of awareness and therefore we cannot readily see it. How can we perceive illness if illness itself is lack of perception. To be ill is to be unaware, to be healthy is to be perceptive, especially of the things that are wrong. When a sick person succeeds in perceiving his illness (and its cause, especially when it's physical) he will then have a chance to overcome it. In this case, having consciousness is being healthy whereas not being aware means being sick.

In other words, illness is the absence of health — a denial, omission or distortion of goodness, of all that is truly real — and being the absence of something means it is merely a flaw. Consciousness does not bring about health, but rather to be healthy is to be conscious; sanity does not come through consciousness, but rather consciousness is sanity.

To be healthy is to see; that is, when we are sane, we perceive things the way they exist — in other words, only a person who is sufficiently healthy can see things as they truly are. How can someone with a vision problem see things correctly? It is for this reason that the deeply pathological fight against their sight, doing everything they can to blind it. To accept consciousness is seeing in order to live; alienation is the avoidance of seeing in order to avoid life.

> *Patient: It's shocking to see how R has not changed, even after all the time he has spent in our community.*
> *Analyst: What do you think about his attitude?*
> *Patient: It seems as if he is quite sick.*
> *Analyst: Or quite blind. R might say he doesn't see his problems, but he cannot say he was acting in harmony with the community in which he lived, and that was why he had to be asked to leave.*

The fundamental question, then, is whether or not a person follows the guidance he receives and then tries to understand the why of it. In any case, to become sane, the person must cooperate — even though doing so may often require an act of faith to believe the orientation of another person.

We can say that seeing is initially perceiving everything that exists — and only after there is that general view is it possible to note the faults that are also there — just as a problem with eyesight is merely a problem in one part of the eye structure. Our enormous difficulty in becoming conscious of our problems lies in the fact that we have abandoned consciousness; therefore it is not a question of our knowing this or that but, rather, of once again accepting the perception of it or not.

> *Patient: RP is always creating difficulties for my work, trying to find out what I'm doing in order to criticize me.*
> *Analyst: What do you think about RP's attitude?*
> *Patient: I think it's envy of my work, an attempt to sabotage it.*
> *Analyst: You need to see that behavior in yourself — how you sabotage your work and then try to put the blame on someone else. You even acquired an illness that prevents you from practicing your profession and then blame the doctors, making your illness difficult to cure.*

Healthcare professionals must be careful when treating individuals who project, because these patients transfer their own ill intentions to those who are treating them and blame the caregivers for their illness.

The well-known Socratic advice to 'know oneself' means that we must overcome an enormous barrier of envy to achieve such knowing. In fact, the envious person sees nothing wrong in himself because when the "feeling" of envy is very strong, it causes almost total blindness.

13 To be healthy is to be interested in what is good; to be sick is to be terrified of seeing mistakes

I have observed that there are two fundamental types of behavior. One is neurotic, in which a person is appalled at seeing any problem and may even become almost completely immobilized, as in a catatonic state. The other is the behavior of people who are committed to their own progress and personal development — who do not allow themselves to be held back by their shortcomings and who persistently try to understand their problems in order to overcome them.

These two types of behavior are opposite; in the one, fear and cowardice predominate; in the other, honesty and ethical attitudes are foremost so that truth and goodness prevail. Only the latter type of personality succeeds in achieving greatness.

The etymological root of the word sanity comes from the Latin word for health (*sanus*): being healthy means healing mistakes, problems, difficulties, illness. Therefore, the word implies continuous action — which is the determining factor in the degree of health an individual enjoys. Similar to the existential philosophers, I believe that we "construct" (re-establish) our own "essence" (structure).

> ▶ *Patient: It shocks me to see how stagnant our society is and with no possibility of changing. I used to think*

> *extraterrestrials could do something to help our planet, but even they don't do anything.*
> ◗ *Analyst: Are you talking about E.T.'s or about yourself?*
> ◗ *Patient: Even if I wanted to do something, I don't have time.*
> ◗ *Analyst: The fact that you're so surprised at the inertia of the E.T.'s shows how shocked you are at the perception of your own immobility. You always expect others to do what you aren't able to do.*

There are two levels of human existence: the sensorial, linked to the senses; and the psychological, having to do with emotions and ideas. When the sensorial predominates, a person may have an oral fixation (food, drink, conversation), an anal fixation (money, social power), or a genital fixation (narcissism, sensuality). However, the underlying factor is always psychological: if bad feelings and thoughts predominate, the person will be dominated by his feelings; but if good emotions and ideas predominate, the person will be normal and enthusiastic about all that is good.

> ◗ *Patient: My ideal was to get married, because I thought being a single woman meant being a failure.*
> ◗ *Analyst: What do you think about marriage?*
> ◗ *Patient: I think it's a way to impress others. At least that's why my mother married my father — for his money.*
> ◗ *Analyst: Money is power in our capitalistic society.*

As we can see, this patient wanted her spouse to take responsibility for all of the major problems in life — and this is true in a great many marriages.

> ◗ *Patient: I got so mad when M said that I want to be poor for the rest of my life.*

> *Analyst: Do you think what she said was true or false?*
> *Patient: True.*
> *Analyst: In your opinion does the truth help or does it create problems?*
> *Patient: It helps.*
> *Analyst: Then you get furious when someone tries to make you accept goodness.*
> *Patient: I never thought I was such an enemy of goodness.*
> *Analyst: That idea shows why there are so few people capable of doing anything perfect.*
> *Patient: Also, I saw that J was doing a bad job on some work he was doing and I didn't call his attention to the problem. It was probably because I didn't want him to do a good job either.*

The purpose of psychotherapy is not to correct mistakes but to bring awareness of ways to deal with them.

> *Patient: I don't know what's wrong with me. I feel very down all the time and I don't feel like doing anything. Even my girlfriend left me!*
> *Analyst: Why do you think she left you?*
> *Patient: She's just that kind of girl.*
> *Analyst: Don't you think that she got tired of your being down all the time? You suffer from tremendous envy which causes you to ruin everything you have.*

I believe that being is sanity, and the rejection of being, illness. If there is a flaw in a person's being, that person will become sick and so will their environment — as evidenced especially by the ecological destruction that is occurring today.

14 Perception is sanity; "imperception" (alienation) is illness

It's important to note that man has made a distinction between knowing and becoming conscious of something, identifying the latter with ethical factors and making knowledge academic, restricted, limited, functioning more as a mask. Because of this, university graduates must learn all sorts of mundane concepts if they are to be accepted into graduate school. The result is a language far removed from reality.

My point is that society has been organized in such a way as to hide the problems which affect something like ninety-percent of its structure. This is why the majority of the people have no idea about what goes on in the halls of power — and those who in fact have social power believe they are invulnerable. In other words, an attitude that constitutes an escape from reality. Any and all perception, no matter how bad the matter, is always good; yet we have built up enormous censorship against consciousness, an attitude that gives rise to all of our many problems. The problem is our blocking of perception; if we did not stifle it, we would not suffer any setbacks. If we were not afraid to know, we would have no difficulty in life. For every awareness we suppress, a mountain of problems ensues.

▶ *Patient: I seem to have lost interest in a lot of things in life, including group psychotherapy.*

The Origin Of Illness

▶ *Analyst: What do you associate group therapy with?*
▶ *Patient: God and truth.*
▶ *Analyst: If you say you reject God and the truth, then you're saying you are interested in the devil and in lies.*

After a few minutes of silence, the patient continued.

▶ *Patient: As incredible as it seems , I guess that's so.*
▶ *Analyst: Another attitude I observe is that you are never firm in your opinion; in your life everything is yes and no, good and evil, health and sickness at the same time.*

Our main problem is our attitude of wanting to ignore consciousness, which practically speaking, is the reason for our existence: life is consciousness, death is unconsciousness. Illness is brought about by our enormous battle against dealing with the problems we ourselves have caused. By trying to escape through pleasurable activities, leisure pastimes and vacations, we overload ourselves with difficulties that make us sick.

▶ *Patient: It really upsets me to see my family sitting on the beach in Bahia doing nothing for a whole week.*
▶ *Analyst: Doing nothing or harming their lives with their alienation?*

We destroy ourselves without perceiving it, because we despise the awareness that does not allow us the freedom to live out our fantasies — and what is even more tragic is the fact that we don't have the slightest perception of the harm we cause ourselves in the process. In short, goodness is synonymous with perception, pathology with its absence, imperception. With perception we do what is good; without perception, we do harm.

15 The most problematic thing about awareness is our failure to perceive goodness

Generally speaking, people spend their lives waiting for something good to come from outside when it already exists inside their being — without their having the slightest idea of this. In other words, consciousness of good is the most difficult thing to accept — because perception itself is one of the greatest gifts of all.

> ▶ Patient: I have to tell my colleagues at work that they're in a destructive pact with one another, jeopardizing our profits, but I don't have the courage to do it.
> ▶ Analyst: What do you associate your colleagues' attitudes with?
> ▶ Patient: With the destruction of the good they have.
> ▶ Analyst: Then you're not aware that you are also destroying the valuable things you possess — just as the others are not aware of all the good they have.

It seems as if our greatest problem today is a lack of consciousness of the good we have received, for in order to see a mistake that is harming us, we must first become aware of the good that exists everywhere. Since we do not deserve all the good things we receive, we also fail to value them as we should.

> *Patient: I notice in Brazil that parents often don't give their children guidance the way they should — opposite to the way children are raised in France, Germany and especially in England and the United States.*

We see that while on the one hand it is not good to censor children, constantly criticizing them for every little thing they do wrong, on the other hand, parents often fail to share important knowledge with their children about things only they can transmit to them, things that are so essential at this time in the children's lives for their future.

> *Patient: I have nothing more to talk about because now I see that my problems are very insignificant.*
> *Analyst: Could it be that, as you mature, you pay less attention to your problems?*
> *Patient: I feel really ashamed to have given so much importance to such trivial things.*
> *Analyst: That's probably because in your life you weren't aware enough of all the good to counterbalance the problems that appeared.*

The point I make here is that awareness of good is fundamental (not to mention the fact that goodness *is* awareness) because, among other things, it obliges us to see the harm we do to ourselves — and at the same time we succeed in seeing what is good, that awareness gives us the confidence to overcome any difficulty.

When we consult a psychotherapist, a counselor or a religious advisor, we are looking for someone to help us resolve our inner conflicts and problems. In psychoanalysis, if the patient has behaved aggressively toward others or depressively toward himself, he is not interested in seeing what he does wrong but rather in finding out how to improve his life and avoid greater problems. In general, we change only when we see that it's in our own best interest to do so.

Key points to remember about censorship

1. Resisting awareness makes us sick.

2. Censorship leads to a lack of awareness, a stifling of affection.

3. The purpose of psychotherapy is to treat resistance and neutralize censorship.

4. Censorship prevents us from recognizing our problems; conscientization is the only way to achieve peace on earth.

5. Blaming problems on "the unconscious" is an attempt to escape from reality.

6. To censor perception leads to illness; to accept perception leads to health. While sanity is perceptible, the cause of illness is not. The challenge in dealing with envy is that we cannot perceive it in ourselves.

7. Sanity is to work to overcome problems in the interest of goodness; illness is to refuse to correct errors and to give in to one's mistakes.

8. Be wary of those who do not accept consciousness.

Part 3

PROJECTION (PARANOIA)

The diagram below illustrates how the person who is not willing to accept any awareness of his shortcomings or problems will, through the process of paranoia, project them onto something or someone else — to the point of becoming psychotic, which is the most serious mental illness of all and the most difficult to treat.

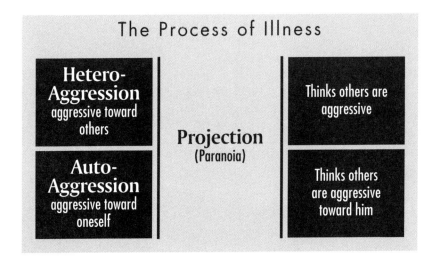

1 Our delusions begin with our projection

If envy is not conscientized, we will automatically project — which means that if we do not see the problem in ourselves, we will transfer it to someone else. This being the case, I believe illness begins with the process of projection, and the greater the projection, the sicker the person. A person who projects is sick; a person who interiorizes is healthy. If I externalize; that is, project what I am (my feelings, thoughts, attitudes, state of mind) onto another person, I am, in fact, inventing a fantasy, a delusion that will be difficult for me to recognize. This is the process by which the mentally ill typically harbor illogical thoughts, ideas out of touch with reality. And it is here that the question of ethics arises, because those who project deny the truth, unwilling to admit how they really are.

> ▶ Patient: I must always be on the lookout for envy. If not, it will completely dominate me.
> ▶ Analyst: Your idea is that you can be totally free of envy.

I propose that envy is the reason why our intellectual life functions at less than ten percent of its capacity. If we allow our behavior to be based on envy, the first consequence is that we practically cut ourselves off from all of the bases for our development (intellectual or otherwise), and thus our value judgments become inverted.

Resistance to seeing problems (our faults, our shortcomings) is directly related to our envy, which we obviously feel deeply ashamed to admit. This is the first consequence of envy; the second is projection, which consists in attributing to someone else what we are loathe to see in ourselves. When pronounced, this second consequence leads to the most serious illnesses (psychoses). With this we complete the infernal triangle of psychopathology.

The process of projection leads to delusional thinking because it eliminates the person's contact with himself. If I perceive the fault to be in another person, then I do not "exist," and if I do not assume responsibility for my own mistakes, then I am free to engage in all manner of destructive behavior.

> ❧ *Patient: I identified with BP in the last group psychotherapy session.*
> ❧ *Analyst: What do you associate BP's attitude with?*
> ❧ *Patient: Projection, being "out of it."*

When we externalize our problems, we lose contact with reality because we are out of touch with ourselves and have no idea what we think. This is why, when someone tries to correct us, we get angry and act like a child throwing a temper tantrum.

> ❧ *Patient: I dreamed I was on a marvelous trip and suddenly a woman jumped out of the moving bus, ruining the trip.*
> ❧ *Analyst: What do you associate the woman's attitude with?*

▶ *Patient: It was envy, wanting to ruin everything.*

We note, then, that envy which is not perceived leads us to ruin our own life or the lives of others — and since envy is the most constant factor of all, we end up, day and night, wrecking our life and the lives of others.

▶ *Patient: I'm very unhappy living with JP.*
▶ *Analyst: What do you think about life with him?*
▶ *Patient: His entire life is dedicated to politics, and it makes me furious.*
▶ *Analyst: Are you envious of his interest in politics?*
▶ *Patient: I believe so.*
▶ *Analyst: So you suffer because of the envy you feel towards him — but you think he is the cause of your suffering.*

We become sick as a result of our envy — and then we blame the person we envy for the suffering we ourselves create.

2 Projection (paranoia) comes from censorship (resistance) against seeing envy (inversion)

There are three steps that lead to illness: a) the process of envy, which produces inversion; b) censorship, which obstructs consciousness; and c) projection, which forges delusions.

> ❱ *Patient: Yesterday, when I came home, my husband was having a fit because our son went to the dentist without his sister.*
> ❱ *Analyst: What happened?*
> ❱ *Patient: Because my daughter wasn't ready to leave, he took the car and went to the dentist without her to teach her a lesson. But my husband got mad at him, not her.*
> ❱ *Analyst: What do you associate your husband's behavior with?*
> ❱ *Patient: He doesn't say anything. He thinks everyone knows what they should do; that they don't need to be told.*
> ❱ *Analyst: Which shows he is harming your daughter by not pointing out her mistakes, doesn't it?*
> ❱ *Patient: His whole family does the same thing.*

The Origin Of Illness

It's important to note that not wanting to point out someone's mistakes to them indicates a strong censorship of consciousness.

> ▶ *Patient: I'm already sort of isolated, but I want to be more so because I think other people mess up my life.*
> ▶ *Analyst: What do they mess up?*
> ▶ *Patient: My ideas and emotions.*
> ▶ *Analyst: Isn't that due to your own self-censorship and repression? Tell me more about these ideas you have.*
> ▶ *Patient: I think people are against me, want to hurt me, etc.*
> ▶ *Analyst: Then you project onto others this attitude of yours against your own life?*

I include this example to caution the reader that the behavior which Freud called the death instinct, in fact has to do with a person's attacking himself — and then projecting the attack onto others, thereby creating unnecessary tension in social life.

Some time later, the same patient said that both S and J had improved a lot because they had become more sociable.

> ▶ *Analyst: So you admit that the acceptance of others is a fundamental condition for growth?*
> ▶ *Patient: I believe so; but one has to accept it.*
> ▶ *Analyst: Whether or not you are accepted is another story. The important thing is the relationship!*
> ▶ *Patient: That's right!*
> ▶ *Analyst: As you can see, any problem comes from projection; that is, from seeing outside yourself something that only exists in your inner self.*
> ▶ *Patient: It's a delusion, isn't it?*

Even after these interpretations the patient abandoned treatment some time later.

> ▶ *Patient: I don't like to see my problems.*
> ▶ *Analyst: Then you think that the knowledge of bad things is harmful, not something good.*
> ▶ *Patient: I'm like a devil.*
> ▶ *Analyst: This is how evil remains covered up and can act freely — and the devil, as you put it — is free to do his work.*
> ▶ *Patient: But he never stops being evil!*
> ▶ *Analyst: In any case, the only way to avoid evil is to recognize it.*

It is easy to see how this patient, by seeing herself as a demon, was strongly censoring the consciousness of her mistakes.

3 Projection takes us outside reality

In the process of projection, we transfer a mental image onto another person as if it were reality, forming a hallucination — and if the projected idea is an aggressive one, the person projecting it enters into persecutory delusions.

> ▶ *Patient: I don't know why LP rejects me so strongly! Or am I the one who is doing the rejecting and blaming him?*
> ▶ *Analyst: Do you see in him how you reject yourself?*

As we see, the process of projection takes a person outside reality: a) because the projection is nothing but a fantasy, or rather a delusion created in the person's own mind; and b) then there is no possibility of a relationship, because the person's thoughts about the other are not real.

> ▶ *Patient: It seems that since I stopped taking tranquilizers, I've gotten worse.*
> ▶ *Analyst: What do you mean?*
> ▶ *Patient: I started thinking about my daughter who went to the United States and I got very sad. She never accepted my love.*

> *Analyst: Do you see what you are projecting onto your daughter? Your own difficulty in giving love, because the medicines you were taking kept your feelings smothered for a long time.*
> *Patient: I realize now that when I was on the medication I didn't feel a thing.*

Note that with our inverted way of thinking, we consider feelings inappropriate, as if they were the cause of mental illness, instead of that it is precisely our censorship of feelings that brings about all psycho-social ills.

> *Patient: I know I shouldn't pick fights with so many people, but some of them I just can't stand.*
> *Analyst: What's important is to become aware of **why** you like or dislike someone, because there is always some prior reason, something you project, that determines your liking or disliking anyone.*

Both knowledge and affection stem from something prior that determines the kind of life a person has, conforming to our essence (love) or to one's projections, the imaginary ideas (delusions) we have of others.

> *Patient (a lawyer): An agreement that one of my clients made with me ended up being disadvantageous for him because he tried to rip me off but didn't succeed. I got totally furious when I discovered his dishonesty.*
> *Analyst: How did he try to rip you off?*
> *Patient: He sold me a lawsuit for $6,000 but then took the case to another lawyer who paid him $11,000 — but he forfeited the $40,000 he would have received.*
> *Analyst: What does that show you?*
> *Patient: That because he was trying to be so shrewd, he*

ended up losing the money that could have been his if he had only waited a little longer.

▶ *Analyst: Are you indignant just about his dishonesty, or because you see that his attitude was detrimental to him, the same as you do to yourself?*

We need to be aware of the fact that paranoia always predominates in the process of projection — in both projective identification and projective idealization — because both are outside of reality.

4 All illness stems from the process of projection

If a theory is not based on reality, it must be considered delusional. I refer here mainly to Sigmund Freud's ideas about incest — considering that the father of psychoanalysis may even have had that problem himself since he was very sick. What I propose is that behavior which stems from the so-called unconscious is sick — which is why a methodology based on the association of ideas is false. I am showing that the cure does not come from the unconscious, but rather by opening oneself to consciousness.

▶ *Patient: I don't feel well.*
▶ *Analyst: Could it be that you are not accepting life?*
▶ *Patient: All I want is to be healthy. The rest will take care of itself.*
▶ *Analyst: No, health comes only if you accept life.*

What really happens is that a negative "feeling" (an anti-feeling) is not perceptible precisely because it is not legitimate. Only the person who has lived according to the truth can later recognize its absence. In other words, only a good individual can perceive evil (destructive attitudes and acts), which becomes the absence of the good he possesses.

The Origin Of Illness

> *Patient: I'm very anguished today. Last night I felt some-*
> *thing dark and scary near me and I tried to ignore it.*
> *Analyst: What do you associate that thing with?*
> *Patient: The power of evil.*
> *Analyst: Do you see that by trying to ignore the evil*
> *that comes from inside you, you become anguished?*

Any and all pathological processes stem from our attitude of not wanting to see that illness comes from our rejection of our own awareness.

> *Patient: (a psychoanalyst) A patient of mine said that*
> *he was very honest but that the government was*
> *corrupt, and then I showed him what the government*
> *(corruption) represents in himself.*
> *Analyst: Why didn't you also tell him that he idealizes*
> *himself a lot?*
> *Patient: I thought that by doing that I would not be*
> *following the analytical technique.*
> *Analyst: If you allow a patient to make an incorrect*
> *association of ideas in this way, it's because you believe*
> *sanity can come from illness.*

I believe that the unconscious is the illness, and not the Freudian idea that the unconscious contains all of the sanity a person needs to heal his illnesses — a sick idea in and of itself!

When a person becomes indignant at the sight of atrocities that others commit, it is because he himself does not want to see his own atrocious intentions. This is why many prosecutors, lawmakers and the powerful have created various ways (the electric chair, lethal injection) to eliminate those who remind them of their own hidden dishonest intentions — showing clearly how they attack others under the protection of the laws they themselves have made.

5 The process of projection (paranoia) is imperceptible

The great drama of projection is that we do not perceive what we are doing, at least not while the projective process is occurring. In other words, we come to believe in what we imagine, in our delusional ideas.

> ▶ *Patient: I identified with AL when the therapy group pointed out that she is very delusional.*
> ▶ *Analyst: What does your identification represent?*
> ▶ *Patient: That I am like her?*
> ▶ *Analyst: Or that you blindly obey your paranoid ideas, just as AL does. You don't only believe in her delusional ideas but in your own as well, which means that you live in a fantasy world.*

It is not hard to see that in the process of projection, not only do we fail to see others as they are but we also fail to perceive our own reality — caught in what British philosopher George Berkeley saw as the impossibility of having contact with reality, believing as he did that the existence of matter and substance were dependent upon the mind. Berkeley foresaw the process of projection.

> *Patient: I was having lunch and my wife began to criticize me for no reason.*
> *Analyst: How do you see her attitude?*
> *Patient: As wanting to put me down.*
> *Analyst: She shows how you always put yourself down.*
> *Patient: I'm always being criticized.*
> *Analyst: It seems as though you even make her berate you so as not to perceive how much you always berate yourself.*
> *Patient: She always threatens separation because she knows I'm dependent on her.*

Note here that the patient was not aware that he projected onto his wife his self-destructiveness.

> *Patient: I notice people don't respect me.*
> *Analyst: What you are noticing is that you don't respect yourself and therefore others don't respect you.*

The more depressive individuals generally project their self-destructiveness onto others, fostering the aggressive behavior of the paranoid type of person — which is why the latter dominate our society, achieving the highest positions of power.

To practice psychotherapy is to treat paranoia. In fact, I believe that projection is an ongoing process of paranoia. However, we must be aware that not only the highly aggressive project. The depressive not only project their destructiveness onto the paranoid but they also feed the aggressiveness of others to avoid seeing their own destructiveness.

6 Pathology is revealed through both projective identification and projective idealization

Projective identification and projective idealization are two sides of the same coin, so to speak. In projective identification we see the other person as inferior, especially if they are a person of value; in projective idealization we see the other as exaggeratedly superior. In both types of projection, we project the idea we have about ourself (inferior or superior). In both cases, we see in the other person our own most serious defects or our own delusional ideas.

People idealize others to the same extent that they idealize themselves; thus, to know how a person sees himself, one need only pay attention to what he says about those he admires. Note, however, that the individual can turn against the one he idealizes and his praise can become contempt. In any case it is important to recognize the geniuses and the saints as being truly exceptional and deserving of praise. In the presence of pathology, what happens is that admiration is generally heaped upon those who do not deserve it.

▶ *Patient: It seems as if I prefer to live more in the world of imagination than in reality.*
▶ *Analyst: Couldn't the world of imagination also be marvelous? Many artists and geniuses live in such a world.*
▶ *Patient: But I'm not an artist!*
▶ *Analyst: Even if you aren't, the universe of imagination*

> *appears to be the route to happiness if it's taken advantage of properly.*

I cite this example to clarify the fact that in the process of psychotherapy, it is absolutely necessary to help patients recapture the marvelous world of their imagination — which they abandoned precisely because of their envy and bad intentions, and especially to enable them to tell the difference between those who are and those who are not persons of worth. Normally, when we admire someone, we know that alongside great value, there are difficulties and problems — and as bad as a person may be, they still have a degree of idealism within them. In the case of deeply pathological individuals, they see others either in a totally idealized way or in a totally negative way — both of these attitudes being equally disagreeable.

Idealization does not exist without identification: the greater the idealization on the one hand, the greater the deprecation on the other.

> *Patient: I always want to give my family things I can't afford.*
> *Analyst: You idealize yourself a lot .*
> *Patient: My husband complains that I want to give my brother too much money, but I believe it will help him straighten out his life.*
> *Analyst: Why do you want to do that?*
> *Patient: My brother is schizophrenic.*
> *Analyst: By doing this aren't you creating a problem with your husband, who supports your brother?*

Note that this patient is practically throwing away the good situation that she has at home by idealizing her brother, her family and herself. Whenever we show exaggerated praise and admiration towards a certain person or country, it is a sign that we harbor the same idealization in respect to ourselves.

7 Both projective idealization and projective identification are delusional

Those who project their idealization easily fall into projective identification: 1) because the process of projection is similar in both instances, and 2) because in both cases we project onto others our delusions (ideas that are not reality-based). Obviously, it is fundamental for us to perceive in ourselves and in others not only the ideals we have, but also the problems. The process of illness begins only when we fail to see ourselves as we are or others as they are. Conflicts begin with projections 1) because the other person is attacked without knowing why, and 2) mainly because the aggressor thinks he has the right to attack because he believes in his delusional projective idea. In fact, it is only those who are seriously unbalanced (insane) who succeed in starting a war.

> ▶ *Patient: I don't understand why WV doesn't tell me what to do about a certain student.*
> ▶ *Analyst: What do you associate WV with ?*
> ▶ *Patient: He's very aggressive and sick.*
> ▶ *Analyst: Then you are really idealizing him. If he never paid any attention to you in the past, why would he do so now?*
> ▶ *Patient: Yes, that's right. I'm imagining he's something that he's not.*

The Origin Of Illness

In this instance it is easy to see how far removed from reality the person who projects their idealization is. Because they do not have a clear idea about the way human beings and reality are, they move easily from one extreme to the other; that is, from idealization to identification and from admiration to disdain, especially in relation to those who are more worthy.

In order to know how sick a person is, one need only verify how greatly they project either idealization or identification. In fact, illness begins with projection, when we see in another person our own ideals or pathology.

> ▶ *Patient: At first, I admired my music teacher a lot, but then I started to reject him, seeing him as my worst enemy.*
> ▶ *Analyst: It's very easy to go from admiration to rejection.*

Note that the pathological personality moves easily from one extreme to the other, from adoration to abomination, from loving to hating.

> ▶ *Patient: I think I'm beginning to understand what you mean by projective identification. When I was in London, I began to despise the people I hung out with, believing they were good for nothing. Now that I'm in Brazil, I idealize the life I had there!*
> ▶ *Analyst: Does idealization make you reject everything you have?*
> ▶ *Patient: I guess I choose delusion because I never accept what I have at the moment! I look down on my friends and colleagues of the moment and admire the ones who are far away. Even in analysis I tried to be something I could never be.*

It is fundamental to perceive that the person who projects (idealization or identification) does not have the slightest contact with himself.

8 Projective identification and projective idealization go hand in hand

The greatest discovery of noted British psychoanalyst Melanie Klein, in regard to treatment, is projective identification, which occurs when we project our own pathological conduct onto another person and then see that person as the cause of our problems. Klein presented a paper in 1946 at the British Psychoanalytical Society entitled "Notes about some schizoid mechanisms" which showed how the child not only wants to destroy its mother, but also to possess her. In this process, the individual sees his aggressive or destructive tendencies in another person (usually in people close to them such as a parent or a spouse) and attacks that person as though they were responsible for all his difficulties.

However, there is another factor that is more subtle and far-reaching: we project our desires onto another person in the belief that we will find in them all that we idealize in life — at the same time believing that what the other thinks about us is what we imagine about ourselves. The conclusion we must arrive at is that first, others are not as we idealize them, and second, others do not perceive us as we truly are. Neither are others how we imagine them to be, nor are we the way others think about us.

In both Klein's projective identification and Keppe's projective idealization there is the same phenomenon of projection (of seeing our own intentions in another person), with the difference that in the former we project our ill intentions and in the latter we project our more noble ideals. In projective identification we see the other as an enemy (which they are not), and in projective idealization we see them as a trusted friend (which they likewise are not).

We can conclude that neither are others what we think, nor are we what others think we are, for better or for worse. If we extend this to humanity, we can conclude that the human race is also not what we believe it to be.

> ▶ *Patient: I think RS is mad at me because I didn't take good care of the telephone she lent me.*
> ▶ *Analyst: What are your ideas about her?*
> ▶ *Patient: I think she's mad because I could have done a better job.*
> ▶ *Analyst: So you are projecting your self-reprimand onto her?*

This excerpt from a session of analysis illustrates how a person projects self-censorship onto someone else — a behavior that Melanie Klein called projective identification, and which is not merely the result of anal-sadistic behavior (as she thought) but mainly an attack against the person's own self. However, at the same time a person engages in projective identification, they also engage in projective idealization, because they project onto the other the exaggerated ideals they have of themselves.

Projective idealization has two aspects: that of imagining the other as being much more perfect than they really are, thus revealing an enormous naïveté; and that of imagining that the other (at least in some cases) has incredible gifts that deserve to be admired. In any case, projective idealization is part of projective identification, but only in the sense of seeing in the other, pathologically, one's highest ideals.

9 Delusions appear in projective identification and in projective idealization

In projective identification, the unbalanced person sees his pathology in someone else, generally in an exaggerated way; in projective idealization, he sees his ideals in another person, also in an exaggerated manner.

> ❱ Patient: When I was remodeling my house, I gave three post-dated checks to the contractor, but he hardly did any work. I went to the house several times to see how the work was coming along, but it looked like he hadn't done a thing.
> ❱ Analyst: What do you think about the attitude of the contractor?
> ❱ Patient: Very dishonest, but my husband should be taking care of it, not me. He always does this and it causes problems for the family.
> ❱ Analyst: Haven't you over-idealized the contractor?

As we can see here, the patient not only idealized the contractor but at the same time placed the blame for her own inaction on her husband — a double delusion. A person can project both identification and idealization with the same intensity at the same time onto two different people, or at different times onto one person. Projection is a delusional way of seeing in someone else not only an illness which that person does not have, but also ideals they do not possess to such a great degree.

> ▶ *Patient: I don't know what happens. I invite people here in the trilogical community to go to the theatre and the movies but no one accepts. But my other friends outside the community always accept.*
> ▶ *Analyst: You project bad things onto your closest friends and good things onto mere acquaintances.*

It is not difficult to see here how the patient projects both his pathological attitudes and his ideals onto others. In other words, he sees his "dreams" in distant acquaintances and his own problems (which he doesn't want to see) in those closest to him.

10 You can tell how unbalanced a person is by how much they idealize

The process of projection is filled with ideas of grandeur and delusions. So much so that the greater a person's idealization, the farther from reality they will be, and conversely, the more realistic a person is, the less they will idealize.

> ❱ *Patient: I went to a concert and the woman next to me started smoking. I asked her to stop but she didn't, so I took the cigarette out of her hand.*
> ❱ *Analyst: What do you associate her attitude with?*
> ❱ *Patient: She was confrontational and arrogant.*
> ❱ *Analyst: Then, using the pollution caused by her smoking as an excuse, you became furious at the awareness she gave you of your own confrontational and petulant attitude?*

Excessive idealization prevents us from accepting life as it is in reality, because it appears too mundane, and instead we live in our delusions of grandeur, which are figments of our imagination.

> ❱ *Patient: I'll try one more year to see if I make money in this job. If I don't, I'm going to quit and do something else.*

The Origin Of Illness

▶ *Analyst: You must pay attention to your intention: whether you truly want to get ahead or not. In order to make money, your decisions have to be based on reality.*

Those who become successful in one type of work will be successful in anything they do, because they focus on reality and avoid delusional ideas.

▶ *Patient: I'm tired of complaining about my husband and now my daughter; I complain about him because he doesn't want to work, and now she is doing the same thing, not getting up in time for school.*
▶ *Analyst: This is a sign that you continue to idealize your husband, and now your daughter as well.*

Apparently the greatest cause of unhappiness in marriage is excessive idealization of one's spouse — which indicates that we also blame our companion for our problems.

▶ *Patient: I got really mad at one of my lawyer colleagues who called me about a deal and later informed me that it would no longer be for $6,000, but only $4,000.*
▶ *Analyst: What do you associate his attitude with?*
▶ *Patient: It's not exactly him, but the company.*
▶ *Analyst: Then what do you think about the attitude of the company?*
▶ *Patient: It's dishonest. They don't want to accept responsibility for the mistake they made.*
▶ *Analyst: Now, what does that attitude signify in you?*
▶ *Patient: Oh! You caught me! I never take responsibility for the mistakes I make! That's why I have this terrible backache! It would be so much easier to accept responsibility right from the start.*
▶ *Analyst: In other words, you're saying that being*

ethical makes life much easier, and that it will even help you avoid having all those physical symptoms.
▶ *Patient: But this is so hard for me to accept! I'm very unhappy with this situation.*
▶ *Analyst: You would like to believe that dishonesty is advantageous — and not that being ethical is what produces well-being.*

It is important to understand that ethical behavior and healthy behavior are one and the same, just as a lack of ethics and sick behavior are one and the same.

▶ *Patient: My singer friend didn't like it when his analyst told him he was bent on ruining his life.*
▶ *Analyst: Do you notice that your attitude is the same?*
▶ *Patient: I can see that attitude in him but I have a hard time seeing it in myself.*
▶ *Analyst: It seems as though one of the main character-istics of artists is their self- destructiveness.*
▶ *Patient: It's a shame that that's the way it is.*

Generally speaking, I can say that when we idealize we have a delusional image about everything, including our-selves — which is why we take two attitudes: first, we adore the one we admire, then attack them ferociously when we are unable to fulfill our delusions of grandeur through the other person.

11 The greater the delusions of grandeur the greater the projective idealization

It is hard to believe that the experts in psychopathology have never paid much attention to the process of idealization, which is a fundamental element in the behavior of those who are the most psychologically unbalanced. Although many psychologists say that neurotic persons do not accept reality even though it is all around them, they (the psychologists) have never explored very deeply the question of how neurotics project onto the world and onto others their delusions of grandeur. It is precisely those delusions that indicate the degree of idealization.

> ▶ *Patient: I don't know what to do now. I don't know if I should retire or do something else.*
> ▶ *Analyst: What do you associate your present line of work with?*
> ▶ *Patient: These days I do almost nothing, but I used to do some very important research.*
> ▶ *Analyst: So you undervalue what is important?*
> ▶ *Patient: I'm just afraid of making too many mistakes.*
> ▶ *Analyst: In that case you don't want to see how many mistakes you make because that would make you have to stop idealizing yourself.*

The Origin Of Illness

The great difficulty many of us have in regard to work is due to our strong idealization of ourselves. Because of this, those who are really sick generally devote their time to reading and study as a way of avoiding contact with the practical side of life. For example, famous theoreticians who merely theorize and have trouble putting themselves into action, do so to protect the grandiose idea they have of themselves. This is why those who call themselves "philosophers" are often considered crazy by the rest of society.

> ▶ *Patient: I miss not having a girlfriend. I was thinking of asking BS or VC for a date but I'm afraid they would turn me down.*
> ▶ *Analyst: Do you see that you idealize life too much, thinking you can have any woman you want at the drop of a hat?*

The miraculous solutions that most people desire show the degree of alienation in which we live. Often, during the course of psychoanalysis, the patient will suddenly join some mystical sect in search of a miracle, or begin some kind of physical treatment (medication, exercise), all of which end up annulling the progress they were making during psychotherapy.

Client JP was calling in for his session of analysis from a public telephone in front of a bank when there was an enormous racket of sirens and helicopters that prevented me from hearing him very well — and the matter he was speaking about was precisely his self-destructiveness.

> ▶ *Analyst: What's going on there?*
> ▶ *Patient: A bank robbery in front of the phone booth.*
> ▶ *Analyst: And you're still there?*
> ▶ *Patient: Just a minute and I'll call you back from another phone.*

When he called back I could still hear an uproar and the patient continued to talk about his destructive tendencies.

> ▶ *Analyst: How come there's still so much noise there?*
> ▶ *Patient: Oh! I'm still pretty close to the bank! I'll call you right back.*

I waited a few minutes and finally the patient called from a quieter phone.

> ▶ *Analyst: Do you see now how you habitually endanger yourself?*
> ▶ *Patient: I guess that was proven just now.*

12 Projective idealization makes a person incapable of accomplishment

With projective idealization we become incapable of self realization in our profession or any other area.

> ▶ *Patient: I've come to really hate doctors. My father was a doctor and everyone looked up to him. My mother was very proud of him and I thought the medical profession had the answer to all human suffering.*
> ▶ *Analyst: Do you think perhaps you idealized doctors and your father too greatly?*
> ▶ *Patient: It seems that society in general has great admiration for the profession. My father, for example, always drove very fast and I was afraid he would kill himself or someone else. I don't know if it's only envy or something else.*
> ▶ *Analyst: In this case you also saw yourself as invincible, believing you could do anything you wanted to.*
> ▶ *Patient: The problem is that I end up admiring other doctors, like the one who did heart transplants at the Clinical Hospital.*
> ▶ *Analyst: You want to keep on idealizing yourself forever, just like society in general does, praising too highly precisely those who idealize themselves the most; that is, those who are the sickest.*

Note here that at the same time the patient admired his father, unconsciously he also desired his death (in a car accident), thus passing from projective idealization to projective identification.

> Patient: *My father recommended that I tell no one about the psychotherapy I'm doing.*
> Analyst: *What do you see in your father's attitude?*
> Patient: *It seems as though he wants to erase all the problems he had and thinks only about the success he could have. My mother told me he goes to fortunetellers.*
> Analyst: *Then does your father idealize himself a lot?*
> Patient: *He always sees himself as being way up there, but my mother is more successful than he is.*

People who idealize themselves greatly see themselves as being extraordinarily productive but in reality they don't produce as much as they think they do. This is why projective idealizers will not subject themselves to psychotherapy.

> Patient: *I notice that in Brazil the parents generally don't raise their children the way they should — different from the way it is in France, Germany and mainly in England and the United States.*

We can see that if on the one hand it is not good to keep after children, correcting them too much, on the other hand parents very often do not give children the important knowledge that only they as guides can transmit at this time in their children's lives — knowledge that is so essential for the children's future. This indicates that the parents think everything will work out by itself — and even that if they don't say anything at all, their children will become balanced individuals on their own. If parents fail to correct their children, it is because the parents suffer from enormous censorship, unwilling to admit any mistakes or anything bad in their life.

13

The sickest people want others to be the way they idealize them

Highly neurotic individuals idealize so much that they are incapable of accepting others as they are. Quick to find or imagine a great number of faults in others, they become unbearable in their relationships. Before neurotic people idealize, they first have a grandiose idea of themselves and then project that idea onto another person, as though the other person is the only one able to understand them. Initially, they may have nice things to say about the other person but then suddenly change their mind and become critical.

> ▶ *Patient: I think I'd better find another girlfriend because the one I have now is irresponsible.*
> ▶ *Analyst: So you want a companion who conforms to your idealization, not to reality. That's why you don't stay with any one of them very long.*

What one notices about the most paranoid individuals is that they want to live out their delusions of grandeur, expecting everyone else to conform to their absurd "idealizations." They are very difficult to get along with because they don't accept living in the real world.

> ▶ *Patient: My work is very inconsistent and as a result I see I can't do anything well.*

> ❯ *Analyst: You're saying that your inconsistency makes you aware that you don't do anything perfectly, like you thought you did.*
> ❯ *Patient: I have so many problems.*
> ❯ *Analyst: Are you realizing that it is only by doing something that a person sees his shortcomings?*

If most of humanity is not as productive as it could be, it is because people live in a state of total idealization — which is the same as saying they do not accept the fact that they have to act in accordance with the reality of life — even though living in accordance with reality brings great satisfaction, as if it were possible to live any other way!

> ❯ *Patient: I get a headache every Sunday.*
> ❯ *Analyst: What happens on Sundays?*
> ❯ *Patient: I spend time with my husband and children, correcting them and giving them guidance.*
> ❯ *Analyst: So this irritates you because you want the entire family to conform to your idealization — and you become annoyed when you see that the world is different from the way you think it should be. This is why family conflicts are so common, sometimes even triggered by just one very sick member.*

14 Action precedes and gives rise to being

If we do not change our behavior, we will stay the way we are today for the rest of our lives. We *are* what we *do*. The Latin dictum "action follows being" (*agere sequitur esse*) is inverted, because in reality "being follows action" (*esse sequitur agere*).

▶ *Patient: I was surprised at the defects the people in group therapy said I have because I don't see them in myself.*

▶ *Analyst: Since you don't do the good things you ought to do, you are not able to recognize the bad things you do.*

The point I make here is that we comprehend only what we do: true understanding and wisdom derive from pure act, while ignorance and illness derive from disturbed behavior. We only perceive what we do, which makes it obvious that we must behave in a healthy way at least some of the time in order to be aware of both good and evil.

▶ *Patient: I don't understand why I ruin my health and my career.*

▶ *Analyst: Reality is revealed through a person's actions, not through knowledge.*

In other words, even our intellect is determined by action and does not grasp all that a person is, because it is only a part of essential act. Thought, then, is a by-product of action, or rather, merely a part of our being. We are what we do; that is, we are identified with the way we act. If a person is affectionate and rational, it is a sign that they are healthy; if they are envious and irrational, it indicates they are sick.

> *Patient: I never really know why I do what I do.*
> *Analyst: Are you saying that knowledge is not always present?*
> *Patient: Yes, I rarely have a clue about anything I do.*
> *Analyst: In that case, you rarely perform what is called a "pure act."*

A distinction must be made between pure and impure acts; that is, between what action really is and what the rejection of it is, because all attitudes of envy, pride, gluttony, greed, anger, laziness and lust are in opposition to (pure) action. It is possible to say then that health derives from action that is good, beautiful and truthful, which in turn determines feeling (love) and knowledge (truth).

15 Don't ruin what is good if you want a good life

We generally copy our parent's behavior, healthy or unhealthy — depending on what suits our own interests.

> ▶ *Patient: My parents only became more well-balanced later in life; however, my oldest brother, who was born when my parents were at their worst, is the most well balanced of all of us.*
> ▶ *Analyst: In that case, he did not imitate your parent's pathology. The healthy part of his personality predominated.*

By denying, omitting or distorting goodness, we behave contrary to the true reality of life — which is an inverted view, seeing what is outside ourselves as good and devaluing our inner qualities.

> ▶ *Patient: When I entered the Boston Conservatory of Music, I was the most poorly behaved student in the class — to the point where I even dropped out. In New York I took school more seriously and then began to have this problem with my fingers.*
> ▶ *Analyst: So in both cases you did not want to study to become a true artist.*

> ❱ *Patient: And that's why I haven't been very successful?*
> ❱ *Analyst: The truth is that you rejected your own development from the start, beginning with the conservatory.*

The idea of psychoanalyst Melanie Klein regarding the need to accept the mother's breast in infancy does not entirely explain the attitude the person may have of self-confidence later in life. In fact, if the child's behavior is one of acceptance during infancy, that in itself is a sign that the process of envy (inversion) in that child is not too great right from the time of birth.

> ❱ *Patient: I don't think I want my life to be bad; but if I don't accept goodness, what else can I expect?*
> ❱ *Analyst: If you do not accept what is good, you will automatically end up with what is bad, because what is bad is merely the denial of the good you failed to accept beforehand.*

In any case, because of our envy, our inverted sense of values, we are displeased by what is good, not by what is bad, for to be displeased with anything bad is a good thing. To take pleasure in what is good is spontaneous and natural, because goodness is inherently pleasant.

1. Projection produces delusional ideas.

2. Projection is a key component of illness.

3. Through projection, a person demonstrates how much they consider themselves to be inferior or superior to others.

4. When a person excessively idealizes others, you can be sure they excessively idealize themselves.

5. One can tell how imbalanced a person is by their degree of projective idealization and projective identification.

6. Identification cannot exist without idealization, projective or otherwise.

7. The human race has chosen the path of pathology; we want the freedom to be crazy and sick.

8. In projection, we see others but we do not see ourselves. We focus our attention on others to avoid seeing ourselves.

ALIENATION - The voluntary but often unperceived attitude of detaching oneself from reality and especially from the consciousness of one's errors. When we are unwilling to accept consciousness of something, we use many different things to alienate ourselves, among them sex, power, money, hyperactivity, travel, television, alcohol and drugs.

ANALYTICAL TRILOGY - A scientific theory and methodology created by Brazilian psychoanalyst Norberto R. Keppe, Ph.D., which unifies the fields of science, philosophy and theology. In the individual this corresponds to the unification of feeling, thought and action that results in full consciousness.

BEING - One's essence, which is fundamentally good, beautiful and truthful.

CENSORSHIP - The prevention of disturbing or painful thoughts, feelings or actions from reaching consciousness except in a disguised form, especially consciousness of psychosocial pathology.

CONSCIOUSNESS - The component of waking awareness, both inside and outside oneself, perceptible by a person at any given instant. Includes awareness of right and wrong, of psychopathological attitudes and of goodness, truth and beauty.

CONSCIENTIZATION - A word coined in English as a synonym for the original in Portuguese used by Dr. Keppe to describe the psychological process of becoming aware of reality, both external and internal, through a mixed process of feeling and knowing.

ENVY - While the dictionary defines "envy" as a combination of discontent, resentment and desire — usually for the possessions, advantages or qualities of another, Keppe adds a new dimension to this definition, broader than ordinary jealousy and closer to the Latin root of the word: *invidere* (*in*=non, *videre*=to see). Keppe sees envy as a psychological blindness, a negation of awareness, an unconscious wish to destroy the goodness and beauty we see not just in others but in our own lives as well. Although Keppe was originally trained as a Freudian analyst, he observed in clinical practice that his patients exhibited envy that was not, as Freud proposed, sexually based. Instead, it was due to a broader rejection of love, an unconscious dismissal of the goodness, truth and beauty in oneself and in others. In Keppe's opinion, envy, although mainly unseen, is the primary destructive psychological force behind all ills — mental, physical and social.

FEELINGS - Keppe proposes that the only real feeling is love, and therefore that envy, hate, anger are not true feelings but primarily attitudes taken against love.

IDEALIZE - To regard or show as perfect or more nearly perfect than is true.

IDENTIFICATION - To recognize in another person one's own characteristics, good or bad. We can identify with someone without realizing it.

INCONSCIENTIZATION / INCONSCIENTIZE - Coined by Keppe to describe the willful attitude of concealing, repressing or denying one's consciousness. Hiding from oneself something one does not wish to see.

INTERIORIZATION - Coined by Keppe to describe the comprehensive process of perceiving the existence of an inner psychological universe greater than our external universe: virtually, the existence in us of the beauty, truth and goodness of the Creator. The most important process in Analytical Trilogy because it constitutes a return to one's inner self, to the source of life and happiness.

INVERSION - A psychological process, first observed by Keppe in 1977 and unique to his work, in which values and the perception of reality are inverted in the individual and in society. Examples: seeing good in something evil and evil in something good; believing that reality, not fantasy, causes suffering; seeing work as a sacrifice and laziness as pleasurable; thinking that love brings suffering and pain; and making wealth, prestige and power the most important goal of all.

NEUROSIS - Any of various mental or emotional disorders involving symptoms such as insecurity, anxiety, depression and irrational fears. According to Keppe, all human beings are neurotic to a greater or lesser degree.

PARANOIA - Irrational distrust of others, delusions of persecution, often strenuously defended with apparent logic and reason.

PROJECT - To externalize or exteriorize (a thought, feeling or action/attitude) so that it appears to have objective reality.

PROJECTION - The unconscious act or process of ascribing to others one's own ideas, impulses or emotions, especially when they are considered undesirable or cause anxiety.

PROJECTIVE IDENTIFICATION AND PROJECTIVE IDEALIZATION are two sides of the same coin, so to speak, in which a person sees in someone else his own most serious defects or the qualities he imagines himself to have. Both types of projection involve unreal, delusional ideas.

In PROJECTIVE IDENTIFICATION, an advanced stage of projection of a person's pathology, the individual sees the other person as being the cause of his problems and unhappiness. The target person(s) is usually emotionally linked to the individual and does not have the problems/attitudes ascribed to him. The sick person generally projects his own defects; that is, sees them in the very person or persons who are good to him. Envy is the underlying cause of projective identification, a theory initially proposed by Melanie Klein.

In PROJECTIVE IDEALIZATION, an even more highly advanced stage of idealization, the person imagines that the object (usually a loved one) possesses ideals and qualities he himself fails to incorporate into himself or his life. Discovered by Norberto Keppe, projective idealization is another expression of envy in the Keppean sense and something that everyone does to some extent, imagining qualities the object does not possess. Very often the projection is an inversion whereby the person sees his own qualities in someone sicker, more unbalanced – exactly the opposite of what occurs in the process of projective identification.

SANITY - Soundness of judgment or reason. Keppe considers a person sane if they are willing and have the humility to accept the consciousness of their envy as well as enough self-control to curb thoughts and actions based on envious impulses. In short, sanity means living and acting in accordance with the goodness, truth and beauty inherent in one's being.

TRUTH - That which is real; that which exists, good or bad. Truth is absolute, the same for everyone, never relative. The same holds true for all untruth, falsehood, lying. For example, spoiled food is not good for anyone; aggression hurts everyone; tyranny is not beneficial for anyone; love is good for everyone; oxygen is good and necessary for everyone.

UNCONSCIOUS, THE - Defined in traditional psychoanalytical theory as the division of the mind containing elements of psychic makeup, such as memories or repressed desires that are not subject to conscious perception or control but that often affect conscious thoughts and behav-

The Origin Of Illness

ior. In Keppe's view, the unconscious exists only as a negation of consciousness, which exists prior to it. He does not consider the unconscious to be an actual "compartment" in the psyche, but sees it as the effort we make to hide our problems, especially our envy. Because our psychopathology is too shameful to admit, we try to ignore it any way we can. As a result, it not only continues to exist but its negative force becomes even greater.

Norberto R. Keppe, Ph.D. is an internationally renowned psychoanalyst, author and founder and president of the International Society of Analytical Trilogy (Integral Psychoanalysis) based in Sao Paulo, Brazil. He trained in Vienna with noted psychoanalysts Victor Frankl, Knut Baumgarten and Igor Caruso. Dr. Keppe created Analytical Trilogy in 1977 after extensive clinical research with thousands of patients. In the 1980's and early 1990's he practiced and lectured in the United States and Europe where he developed his work on socio-pathology and metaphysics. Back in Brazil in 1997, he developed the Psycholinguistic Therapeutic Method for Education, which enables students to overcome emotional blockages that interfere with learning. He is the author of numerous books which have been translated into eight languages

For additional information and to purchase books, tapes and videos about Analytical Trilogy by Norberto R. Keppe and other authors in English visit the web site: http://www.analyticaltrilogy.org

Join the Analytical Trilogy Book Club meeting weekly via teleconference. Participation is free and open to all. Read chapters from Dr. Keppe's books and discuss them with people from across the US and Canada. For registration and information see www.analyticaltrilogy.org .

Also by Norberto R. Keppe

English translations
Liberation
Glorification
The Decay of the American People (and of The United States)
Liberation of the People – The Pathology of Power
Work and Capital
Trilogical Metaphysics I - The Liberation of Being

Original Portuguese editions
O Homem Universal
A Nova Física da Metafisica Desinvertida
Metafísica Trilógica I - A Libertação do Ser
Metafisica Trilógica II - Fenômenos Sensoriais "Transcendentais"
Metafisica Trilogica III - Cura Através das Forças Energéticas
A Libertação da Vontade (A Libertação do Livre Arbítrio)
A Libertação Pelo Conhecimento (A Idade da Razão)
Sociopatologia (Bases para a Civilização do Terceiro Milênio)
Trabalho & Capital
A Glorifição
A Libertação
A Libertação dos Povos – A Patologia do Poder
A Decadência do Povo Americano (e dos EUA)
O Reino do Homem - Volumes I e II
Contemplação e Ação
Trilogia
A Consciência
Auto-Sentimento
Psicanálise da Sociedade